STUBBOR

MW00456403

Fresh Inspiration from Ancient Women

Janet Creps

To Jamie,
Thanks for all you are!
you do who you are!
you are a true blessing & gift
from God
Love & hugs
Janet

ACKNOWLEDGEMENTS

There are no words to express my gratitude to those who have made this book possible. Writing truly is a team effort, and my team has been my husband Earl, my editor, proofreader, and a network of supporters including friends, family, and co-laborers in Christ.

I extend my thanks to my editor and friend Lois Olena who, in spite of her countless responsibilities, sacrificed her time and effort to help make this book so much better than it would have been otherwise. My amazing proofreader, Abby, made many insightful and invaluable suggestions, and countless improvements to the final text.

To all of my supporters who were a continual source of encouragement to me in this year-long writing journey…you know who you are…Thanks so much!

Most of all, I am deeply indebted to my husband Earl who has been a significant help as an editor and an encourager in the times when I felt like giving up.

Needless to say, I am forever grateful to Jesus who gave me a new life, and forever exists as our only hope—not only for abundant life on earth, but life everlasting.

Thank you all.

© 2018 Janet Creps
ISBN: 9781983199707

CONTENTS

Introduction

Hope Wanted

"For whatever things were written before were written for
our learning, that we through the patience and comfort of
the Scriptures might have hope"
(Romans 15:4 NKJV).

I'm relaxing in a canvas lawn chair on our back deck
while basking in the warm sunshine, surrounded by urns of
multicolored rose bushes. The towering pines and cedars
occupying the plateau on which our property rests take my
breath away. Gazing at the beautiful forest setting fills me
with life. Watching a finch flutter about the rock garden in
front of me, I'm wondering: *How did I get here?*

Not long ago, I was living in a city where the front door
of my home was only a few yards from a busy sidewalk. The
"scenic" view from our front window was a worn-down
apartment building across the street where we observed the
occasional drug deal. The soundtrack of our life was
composed of police sirens, barking dogs, and the bellowing

of domestic disturbances. Our neighborhood fostered an environment of drugs, prostitution, and murder.

Now, the biggest threat we face is the occasional black bear drifting out of the trees and into our backyard.

However, my new peaceful surroundings did not offer an immediate cure for my broken heart. When I arrived in Washington State, my life resembled the shattered Japanese china cup sitting in our dining room hutch, one of the casualties of our move. The cup is too fragmented to glue together, but too precious to throw away. All things considered, I am grateful to have moved to Washington in one piece with only minor physical injuries. Compared to the variety of challenges and crises other people have faced, my experiences seem like a day at the beach.

My emotional bruises came along with me and our truckload of furniture on the 800-mile drive from the East Bay to our new address in western Washington. They serve as painful souvenirs of a difficult ministry experience starting a church.

If you meet me, you may notice the small bump on the top of my nose—a reminder of a fall on a sidewalk where I landed on my face. Moreover, the titanium brace in my left arm is a small token of the surgery required after fracturing my elbow on my first urban bicycle ride.

The cause of my broken condition was more than just minor injuries or chronic fatigue. I was the casualty of a car wreck level of disappointment. Our church start-up in the Bay Area of California came close to a breakthrough, only to lose momentum slowly. We ended up with only three or four committed congregants in an empty auditorium. All of our congregants were involved in some part of the service.

What happened? I invested years of energy and even gave away my heart... for what? To end up with three people? It seemed to me that our every attempt at "doing church" — organizing events, teaching, preaching, leadership training, small groups, and more importantly one-to-one personal ministry — was all in vain.

As if holding church services in an empty room was not bad enough, nothing else seemed to go well either. It felt as though everything I touched died — even the roses in my backyard! They had plenty of sunshine, but despite my diligence in watering them and keeping them free from fungus and diseases, they failed to flourish under my "ministry."

These demoralizing experiences took their toll on my faith. I felt spiritually anemic. My soul was malnourished from a long, dry season of unanswered prayers. My heart felt numb from grieving the loss of dreams I once envisioned for our (I should say God's) ministry and our city.

I could only arrive at one conclusion to explain the failures that seemed to mock me every time I visited a thriving church near our city: God doesn't like me. If He does, He is doing a poor job of letting me know.

Did I make some mistakes? Are there things I would do differently if I could do it all again? Absolutely! However, addressing these issues would involve another book.

In spite of everything, I somehow held on to the core of my Christian beliefs. I felt as though my hands were grasping the ledge of a towering cliff and my strength weakened a little more each day. Through God's grace, I believed that Jesus is real and that God's simple message of love has come to us through His son. This truth was all that remained of my once passionate faith.

Consequently, following years of failed attempts at restarts, vision-casting, and church growth strategies, a door opened for us to make a move and we took the opportunity without much hesitation.

My recent move to Washington offered me more than simply a break from church life and the new perks of being surrounded by thick forests, great coffee, and scenic mountain views. This relocation would soon become for me the ultimate test of my faith: whether or not I believed God had anything promising in store for my future.

For this reason, I launched out on an adventure of hope. My search became the inspiration for this book. As long as we have hope, we can make it through anything.

I believe the story of God's love is filled with His promises to lift us out of despair and fill us with faith. He has made His plans toward us clear. They are "thoughts of peace and not of evil, to give you a future and a hope" (Jeremiah 29:11).

I have to confess that the temptation exists to think this promise, while true in principal, does not apply to my situation. Perhaps I am the exception to the rule. Perhaps somehow I missed getting in line when God was generously passing out His love, favor, and blessings. In the 2003 film, *The Matrix Reloaded,* a character known as The Architect describes feeling of hope as "the quintessential human delusion, simultaneously the source of your greatest strength, and your greatest weakness."[1] Hope is either the world's biggest truth or its biggest lie. I knew this dilemma well.

I am likely not on this journey alone. People are crying out for something deeper than relief from their personal crises and something more than problem-solving skills or strength to navigate through personal struggles. Ultimately, we need something bigger than the ability to handle today's problems. We need to grasp the deep assumption and high expectation that, regardless of what happens to us, we will succeed, rise up, and conquer.

Many Christians have endured so much disappointment that they live in near despair. Life has taken the wind out of their sails, eaten away their confidence, and even stunted their creativity. They are afraid to dream again.

The side effects of this kind of discouragement affect us on so many levels. Some struggle with relationships. I have listened to many single young women, for instance, pour out their longing for a healthy relationship with a member of the opposite sex. Cries for hope flood the Internet every minute. Lonely people plead for love and intimacy through social media or porn. Others are facing problems with their careers, marriages, or children. For many, despair lurks just a news flash away as the long list of school shootings and other tragedies never seems to end.

While writing this book, my life was interrupted by a family emergency. I made an unexpected trip to Anchorage for the funeral of my niece who suddenly ended her life at the age of 29.

No one saw it coming. She had become overwhelmed by the stresses of her life and the complexity of her problems and saw no way out.

At the service, a sequence of slides with pictures of our niece flowed across the screen as recorded violin music played softly in the background. The depth of our family's aching grief was temporarily disguised in an endless barrage of conversations. Some conversations were about last minute details of the service. Others took place around the tables during the reception. Many sought for meaning and spiritual solace.

It was not difficult to discern what many people were thinking: *Why did she take her life? What could I have done to stop her?* Most of all, they were probably wondering where her hope ended and tragedy began.

This sad experience leads to the critical launching point of this book. At some point, we all find ourselves asking questions about hope. How we answer them defines us.

Hope flourishes in the personal stories of those who discovered it and lived it. What better way to embrace this phenomenon than through the powerful narratives found in Scripture? My journey to find hope led me to the courageous women of ancient times described in the Bible who have blazed the trail of hope before me — women like Ruth, Sarah, and Anna, to name a few. Through the rollercoaster ride of their experiences, each of these remarkable women can become our teacher and our inspiration towards a new way of life.

These are stories of women who found what I call "stubborn hope." I borrowed this term from author Anne

Lamott, who describes it this way: "Hope begins in the dark, the *stubborn hope* that if you just show up and try to do the right thing, the dawn will come. You wait and watch and work: You don't give up."[2]

These women of the Bible were by no means perfect, nor did they live like spiritual giants. However, they had something inside: the grace of God in their hearts that would not let go. Some found hope simply by not giving up. Others found it after a lifetime of discouragement. Some found it in the midst of tragedy. God used some as an instrument to bring hope to others. In each case, God's grace enabled them with a new vision and a revelation that provided them with a new way of life.

This book is dedicated to these remarkable women who discovered the power of stubborn hope. These are among the many women in whom God's illustrious story of hope has played out. These women didn't give up, and God refused to give up on them.

My purpose in this book is not to take you on a cathartic tour of the trials in my life or to use the reader as an outlet for processing my own experiences. This book is *for you*. Together, we will take a journey through the lives of these remarkable women. Along the way, we will look for hope together.

The Scriptures demonstrate hope through those who lived it, those who struggled to find it, and ultimately the Person who embodied it when He walked this earth. I call these amazing women the champions of stubborn hope. I want to be among them. I believe you will too. These are their stories.

1

THE WOMAN WHO WOULDN'T LEAVE

Hope Insists

"Then He spoke a parable to them, that men always ought to pray and not lose heart." (Luke 18:1 NKJV)

Have you ever craved an Egg McMuffin? A longing for that sandwich came over me one morning heading west on Interstate 44 on my way to Dallas in our red Mazda LX. The urge for a warm, toasty #Englishmuffin/Canadianbacon/toppedwithafriedegg/smotheredwithmeltedcheese is totally irresistible! I can almost smell it as I write this paragraph.

Having been on the road for almost five hours, I was getting hungrier by the minute when, at last, there was the exit ramp to a McDonald's only a couple of miles ahead. When I got off the highway and into the parking lot, I realized this was not the typical building associated with the franchise. This was my first "Mega" McDonald's! It was a mammoth two-story structure built like a highway overpass, with a staircase to the food area on the second floor.

I didn't mind waiting in the long line for my turn to order. I knew that satisfying my extreme hunger for the glorious muffin would be well worth the inconvenient delay in my trip.

To my disappointment, however, I discovered this was the worst McDonald's ever! I was totally unprepared for the tension-filled conversation with the person at the counter. It did not go well:

Me: "One Egg McMuffin and one small coffee to-go, please."

Crewmember: "We stopped serving those (the McMuffins) at 10:30." (It was 10:45. I was only fifteen minutes late.)

Me: "Well, can't I buy one that's leftover?" (I could see two still sitting there near the counter.)

Crewmember: "No, we stopped serving them at 10:30."

For those loyal McDonald's customers, you must keep in mind this occurred before the restaurant began serving them all day. Who knows? Perhaps I had a role in changing the course of breakfast history at McDonald's!

I powered through every people skill I could muster: smiling, being reasonable and kind, showing respect, using eye contact, even trying shameless false humility and bribery (actually that never happened) with no success.

It wasn't my intention to hold up the line, yet the more the crewmember refused to cave in, the greater my craving grew. I thought to myself: *This is unfair.* I realize now that I sound like a whiny, ungrateful, spoiled child whose unreasonable mother refused her an extra chocolate chip cookie before dinner. Poor Janet! She didn't get her McMuffin! However, I'm not alone.

Jesus was well aware of the blunt reality that life is unfair. In one of His parables, He tells a compelling story about a conflict between a powerless widow and a corrupt judge. The woman who believed she was treated unfairly asked this judge for only one thing: justice. She can see the extra Egg McMuffin. It's sitting right on the shelf! It's not fair that she shouldn't have it! This poor woman is not getting the righteous treatment she deserves. Yet the arbitrator refuses to acknowledge her plight and ignores her continual pleas for what was entitled to her.

When we feel we are not getting the justice or the answers we deserve from God, our lives can often parallel the relationship between the unfair judge and the widow.

Why does "simple" faith seem so complicated? How do I navigate this unwelcome tension between my reality and my faith, when what I need from God does not match my experiences? It is difficult to know how to respond when the results we anticipate from our prayers do not line up with the reality of our lives — similar to how I felt when I was denied the extra McMuffin I saw sitting on the shelf.

If you have wrestled with these issues in your faith, you are not alone. Jesus came to shed light on all of the shadows of our doubts. His story about the judge and the widow offers powerful insights about prayer and fairness. Perhaps you are familiar with this parable and have read it countless times. I believe it's still worth taking another look.

Let's start at the beginning of Luke's account: "Then He spoke a parable to them, that men always ought to pray and not lose heart" (Luke 18:1). In its original context, the phrase "lose heart" refers to being negatively influenced with the *outcome* of experiencing inner *weariness.*"[1]

Trials make you tired! Jesus understood the physical and emotional fatigue people experience when facing roadblocks in their faith. Nevertheless, He encouraged His followers to continue to pray even when they grew weary.

In this parable, the characters become our teachers. Each personality shows us something remarkable about the character of God. As the story unfolds, all three individuals play their part in the drama of hope, offering insight into overcoming the battle of faith versus doubt.

Let's begin with the first character on the scene: the judge. "There was in a certain city a judge who did not fear God nor regard man. Now there was a widow in that city; and she came to him, saying, 'Get justice for me from my adversary. And he would not for a while'" (Luke 18:2-4).

What do we know about this judge? He probably was not Jewish. Ordinary disputes between Jewish people were taken before the elders, and not into the public courts. The fact that only one judge was involved in the widow's case may indicate the dispute was a financial matter.

We know from the story that this judge "neither feared God nor regarded man" (Luke 18:2). Perhaps he was one of the paid magistrates appointed by the Romans or their officials. Historically, these arbitrators were notorious for corruption. According to one scholar, "Unless a plaintiff had influence and money to bribe his way to a verdict he had no hope of ever getting the case settled, these judges were said to pervert justice for a dish of meat."[2] Or, could we say an Egg McMuffin.

Jesus' words, "And he would not for awhile" (Luke 18:4), demonstrate the judge's heartless behavior toward the helpless woman. The judge's message to the widow is unmistakable: "Go away! Leave me alone!" He brushes her off as though he were swatting at an annoying fly. To him, she is the equivalent of having unwelcome visitors at your house who never leave. Of course, the judge may want a bribe, and he knows she has no money. If we were to play out this scenario as a modern-day drama in a hamburger franchise, the judge could say something like "You are wasting my time." He would insist: "We stopped serving McMuffins at 10:30. Go away!"

I can relate to those individuals who have been "sent away." We once were looking into a new location for our church, and came upon a spacious, modern theater for rent by a prominent firm. The auditorium was ideal for our congregation. It was conveniently located in the downtown of our city and the perfect size for what we needed. I made several attempts to contact Sandy, the realtor who was listed with the property, with no success. Finally, it happened. After two weeks of silence, I received a call from her informing us to make an offer on the property for her clients to consider.

Immediately we jumped on it with what we considered a generous offer. We waited patiently for several days for a response, but never heard back. Finally, I contacted Sandy, who broke the bad news. The owners had turned us down with a firm "No."

The reason she gave? The offer was not even close to

matching what the firm could demand in our high-priced real estate market. That's what I believed at first. However, the firm's true reason was that they didn't want to rent their property to a church. In other words, they told us: "We don't want a church here." Thus, like the reluctant judge in the parable, their message was clear: "Go away!"

What can we learn from the judge in this story? For some, God can seem like the unfair judge — especially during times when we see little evidence that He has heard our prayers. Often, "the judge" in our life sends us away by telling us lies about the character of God — that God is just like the unfair judge, unwilling and unsympathetic to our problems. If He was sympathetic, He would give you the "Egg McMuffin" you are hungry for, or that fabulous building ideal for your church. The judge tells you that God isn't listening. He doesn't care about you. You are wasting your time praying to Him. The judge tells you your situation is too tough for God. Even worse, for those who are living a life of despair, the judge will tell you that, because of your problems or the mistakes in your past, you are beyond hope. You might as well go home.

Once you are told to go away, it becomes even more difficult to take another chance or another risk. You may be familiar with the comic strip character Charlie Brown, who evolved into the *Peanuts* commercial franchise with all of its advertising, animated movies, holiday films made for television, and more. One of the most familiar scenes in the comic strip and its companion TV program involves Charlie Brown's friend Lucy holding a football in front of him, taunting him to run toward her and kick the ball. Each time Charlie runs to kick the football, just as he approaches it, Lucy quickly snatches it away. The pitiful pattern of Lucy's deceit and Charlie Brown's failure to kick the ball is a staple throughout the life of the comic strip. Regardless of the pattern, Charlie Brown never gives up. He keeps falling for the same routine over and over again.

Life can feel like Lucy is holding the ball for you, and just as you are about to give it a big kick, she pulls it away. You land on your back, while Lucy laughs. It's easy to allow yourself to believe this is the life God has planned for you: endless futility.

The story Jesus shares, however, takes a radical turn. The conflict between these two individuals, the judge and the woman, is not over. In fact, it is just beginning. Let's turn our attention away from the judge to a more important player in the story: a defenseless but relentless widow.

Now there was a widow in that city; and she came to him, saying, 'Get justice for me from my adversary.' And he would not for a while; but afterward he said within himself, 'Though I do not fear God nor regard man, yet because this widow troubles me I will avenge her, lest by her continual coming she weary me' (Luke 18:3-5).

Imagine being a widow in first-century Israel. In the Gospels, widows were known for their deeds of kindness. They were also not necessarily elderly. The woman in the story could have been a young girl; in ancient culture, women married in their early to mid-teens because life expectancy for men was only the mid-thirties.

Moreover, widows were among the most vulnerable people in society. According to commentator William Barclay, "The widow was the symbol of all who were poor and defenseless. It was obvious that she, without resource of any kind, had no hope of ever extracting justice from such a judge."[3] And yet, God cared about widows and required that His people provide for these women. Scripture offers several examples of God executing justice for widows by supplying them with food and clothing. Furthermore, in the New Testament, Jesus showed kindness and compassion toward women, often elevating them from the lower economic classes of society.

Thus, it is no surprise that Jesus chose to use a woman from a marginalized people group to become our teacher.

What can we learn about prayer from this remarkable woman? What was her secret for getting what she needed?

She never gave up. She was aware of the key to getting the judge's attention: determination. You can sense her tooth-gritting doggedness in the judge's words in Jesus' story: "Though I do not fear God nor regard man, yet because this widow troubles me I will avenge her, lest by her continual coming she weary me" (Luke 18:5).

Hope insists. This woman refuses to be denied. She insists on having what was owed to her. She holds onto her stubborn hope — a brand of hope that takes action, walks, talks, and refuses to take "no" for an answer.

Contrary to the judge's message ("Go away!"), the message of the widow is "Don't give up!" Hope demands a hearing.

Persevering in prayer does not involve barking orders at God, hoping He will bend to your commands. Perseverance flows from having faith that God is at work in your life.

I took a brief break from writing this chapter to plant a couple packages of tulip bulbs. Tulips are lovely, but bulbs are not. They resemble large garlic cloves with a paper-thin, brownish skin. The bulbs should be planted four or five inches deep during the fall or early winter in order to see them bloom in the spring.

This experience provided new insight for me into how

prayer works in our lives. Like hope, prayer is about planting something. An amazing transformation happens when small, ugly bulbs planted deep in the earth blossom into a colorful carpet of bright beautiful flowers. At first they seem dead in the dirt, but later life springs up!

I believe prayers work in a similar manner. Plant your petitions to God deep in the soil of your life, and wait for the miracles to bloom. Prayers, like planting tulips, serve as investments in your faith. Your prayers make a difference! Think of every prayer to Jesus as an investment in your spiritual walk, a miracle in the "bulb" state.

This means good news ahead for discouraged people who are diligently burying prayer bulbs in the dirt. For the widow, her petitions came into full bloom. As Jesus' story unfolds, the judge's resistance is weakening. We soon discover that the widow's persistence wore the judge down. Although he wanted her out of his way, he is left with no option but to give in: "but afterward he said within himself, 'Though I do not fear God nor regard man, yet because this widow troubles me I will avenge her, lest by her continual coming she weary me'" (Luke 18:4-5).

The powerful truth this woman brings to the story is a simple one: don't give up. Contrary to the judge' commands to go away, the widow encourages us, "Keep coming back."

Like the judge and the widow, the voices of both hope and resistance speak to us quite clearly at the crossroads of our circumstances. We are metaphorically stopped at an intersection where the traffic light's red and green signals glow at the same time. The two opposing messages meet at the crossroads of hope. The judge tells us "Go away" while the widow encourages us: "Don't give up."

The Apostle Paul recognized this battle in his letter to the Corinthian church: "For the Son of God, Jesus Christ, who was preached among you by us—by me, Slivanus, and Timothy—was not Yes and No, but in Him was Yes. For all the promises of God in Him *are* Yes, and in Him Amen, to the glory of God through us" (2 Corinthians 1:19-20).

In Him is Yes! Even though we were turned down for the theater, God opened a door for our church to meet in an office building in downtown after several additional "No's." The realtor who listed the office space laughed at the possibility of our church being able to afford such a place, but it wasn't long before we broke down the "judge" and the owner let us rent it for 60 percent less than market value. Soon we were holding services in the very space that was supposed to be impossible.

Though the judges may be against you, keep in mind that God is pulling for you. Many times in the Gospels, Jesus contrasts God's love and compassion with both nature and human behavior, followed by questions about faith. We have witnessed the behavior of a reluctant judge and the persistence of a desperate widow, but the story is not over. The most important personality of all has yet to arrive on the scene. At the puzzling juncture between faith and doubt, the paramount game changer in this narrative appears as the One telling the story — Jesus.

Jesus ends the parable with transforming good news for all who may be struggling with their faith: "I love you." He reveals not only the moral of the story, but also how His compassionate nature expresses His love to all who cry out to him.

In the end, Jesus meets us at the intersection of reality and our faith, between what we think we need and what we feel we have. He is larger than our prayers, bigger than our faith, our confusion, and even our doubts. He promises, "And shall God not avenge His elect who cry out day and night to Him...I tell you that He will avenge them speedily" (Luke 18:7-8).

Jesus closes the gap we perceive between our prayers and our unmet needs. He meets us in this very place where we are struggling to see Him. Jesus reassures us that His generosity knows no bounds: "If you then, being evil, know how to give good gifts to your children, how much more will your Father who is in heaven give good things to those who ask Him!" (Mathew 7:11).

The characters in the widow's narrative lead us to the truth of who Jesus is, reminding us that God is love, and that He longs for us to seek Him in order to experience His love for us. Ultimately, the primary reason to persevere in prayer is because Jesus wants to be with us. Prayer offers an opportunity to spend time in His presence. He enjoys our company.

I grew up in a small town in chilly northwest Wisconsin. My father worked as a commercial artist in the advertising department of a company located near our house. We were far from wealthy. We lived in an average, undersized ranch home with only one full bathroom available for a family of six children. We had one unique substance, and we had more of it at our disposal than anyone in town. We had *paper*—reams upon reams of it supplied by the company for which my father worked. His office was full of metal shelves piled with a wide assortment of paper in every size and color. He kept a stash of paper at the house that could fill a boxcar. We could have been featured on the reality show *Hoarders*—but only with paper. Our basement was cluttered with piles of unused construction paper in all different colors and weights.

This mammoth inventory of paper motivated my artistic tendencies. I was free to take risks. I could use as much paper as I wanted because the supply seemed infinite. There were no conditions. If I didn't like a picture I drew, I could just throw it away like yesterday's trash. There was more paper than I could use in a lifetime—an inexhaustible inventory!

When Jesus uses the phrase, "How much more," I cannot help but think about that endless supply of paper filling my childhood. Jesus is offering an infinite, eternal supply of himself. During those times when I find myself discouraged, I must remember the "how much more" of Jesus that is available to meet my every need. I think about how generous He is and how much He loves me, and that gives me faith that He is working His plan and purpose in my life.

He is ready to come to the aid of all those "who cry day and night to Him." Follow the widow's advice. Trust Him. Keep praying. Keep planting. New life will spring up.

A Prayer

Lord, you are so much more, so much greater than all my prayers and all my needs!
Thank you for being attentive to the desires in my heart as I cry out to you.
You do not send me away like the reluctant judge,
but instead you care so deeply about everything that concerns me, whether big or small.

Thank you, Lord, for giving me the faith I need to keep

seeking Your face

even when at times I feel weary and helpless.

Help me to focus on the boundless love you have for me.

Thank you, Father, for your awesome presence

in every place of doubt in my fragile faith.

Questions for Reflection

- Reflect on a specific time when you heard "No!" from a "judge" in your life. How did you react to it?

- Read Matthew 7:7-12 - What need have you been praying about the most? What would you advise someone in your situation to do?

- Read 2 Corinthians 1:17-24, Romans 8:31-32, 37 - What do these scriptures tell us about God's heart toward us in our circumstances?

2

RUTH

Hope Begins

"Your people *shall be* my people, And your God, my God."
(Ruth 1:16 NKJV)

Have you ever experienced a crisis that changed your life? Just ask a close relative of mine. I'll call her Emily. Her husband Don left for a trip to northern Wisconsin to enjoy his favorite pastime, fishing, and never made it back home. On his return trip to Illinois, he fell ill and a trauma helicopter flew him to a nearby hospital. Only days later, he died of a brain aneurism at the age of 55.

Losing a spouse tops the list of stressful life events. I am unaware of any resources that can adequately prepare someone for the devastating shock of becoming a widow.

As if the trauma of losing her spouse wasn't difficult

enough, Emily was suddenly single. The life she had once known as a happily married woman had instantly disappeared. Emily describes her experience:

Before Don's death, we both worked many hours and that left us with very little free time. I saw my job as taking care of him by providing for his needs. I loved doing this and never tired of his company.

This is what comprised my identity. I was the person behind the scenes and the one giving support through prayer and physical care. I had a few other hobbies like art, reading, and gardening. I always believed I would do these hobbies when I retired, and deep inside, I believed I would do those things with my husband when we would have time together in a few years.

AFTER Don's death I immediately was disconnected from ALL of those roles. I was no longer married, no longer a pastor's wife, no longer behind him each day, and no longer a part of his work community. Documents I would sign called me a "widow," even though I am still the same person. (I hate that title!) I remember feeling like my life was a large jar of confetti that had been dumped out.

Emily was about to embark on a journey of reinventing herself. As a newly single woman, she faced a complicated road ahead which required fresh strength, God's healing grace, and a different way of doing life.

Emily is not alone. Countless others have gone before her.

You may be familiar with a woman from the ancient Middle East named Ruth, who is known for her strength of character and godly virtues. Ruth found herself in a situation similar to Emily's.

Ruth's story begins as she is living in a region once known as Moab, on the eastern shore of the Dead Sea. A Moabite by birth, she marries into a Hebrew family. Shortly after, multiple sudden tragedies claim the lives of three members of her family. Ruth's husband dies, the spouse of her sister dies, and her father-in-law dies. All three are gone, all at once. At this critical juncture in her life, Ruth is forced to make a difficult decision. Will she follow the pleas of her Hebrew mother-in-law, Naomi, and return to her homeland in Moab with her also-widowed sister? Or should she go to Bethlehem with Naomi and risk leaving her comfort to become a stranger in a foreign land? Contrary to her mother-in law's plea for her to return to Moab, Ruth is determined to remain with Naomi and step out into the great unknown.

"Your people *shall be* my people, And your God, my God," she insists. Now what? Ruth is about to enter a strange land where she has no friends, relatives, or people of her ethnicity. Like Ruth, there are times when we find ourselves living in the "Now what?" zone. "Now what's" are those unwelcome occasions where circumstances beyond our control invade like uninvited guests in our seemingly ordinary lives. A "Now what?" scenario is not limited to unforeseen tragedy. This dilemma can accompany a variety of unfamiliar life experiences, such as a new job or career, a move to a new location, getting married, or even having one's first child.

You know you have arrived in your "Now what?" zone when you find yourself totally unprepared in an unfamiliar environment. I have experienced this on many occasions when travelling outside the United States. My husband, Earl, has this annoying habit of abandoning me at social events, especially meals. He will often leave the table for long periods of time to chat with friends, take photos, or make calls. On one occasion, he left me alone at a restaurant table in Tokyo with several Japanese pastors who did not speak English. Earl and I were on a mission trip when our host arranged for us to have lunch with pastors in the area. Without consulting us, our host decided he would not attend, so I was the only English speaker at the table when Earl stepped away. He was only gone for a few minutes, but it felt like an eternity of awkward.

Sometimes, "Now what?" is the first thought in your mind when walking into a room full of strangers. During our season in Berkeley, California, we became members of the Chamber of Commerce in order to develop relationships within our frequently standoffish urban community. Our commitment involved attending events like breakfasts and open houses with several dozen business professionals. It felt weird and often embarrassing to come up with clever ways to initiate conversations, especially when a person would politely move on to talk with someone they found more important or interesting than me.

Strange experiences in restaurants or rooms full of strangers cannot begin to describe the difficulty of significant life transitions. I am not unfamiliar with this challenge, as we have recently relocated from our intensely urban Bay Area home to the wooded Seattle suburbs where my husband embarked on a new position at a local university. The move was like a cultural moon landing—a long trip to a totally different setting.

Like Ruth, you may find yourself in very unfamiliar surroundings far from your friends and family, where every face looks like a stranger. You may be left with the daunting question: *Where do I begin?*

Ruth and Naomi's journey involved trekking through at least thirty miles of steep, rugged mountainous terrain. On a clear day with decent roads, I could make a trip like this in less than two hours in my old Volvo C-30. Imagine, however, what a journey like this would entail on foot thousands of years ago. I wonder how they carried all of their belongings? How weary these women must have grown during their long, arduous journey. Biblical scholars estimate the trip would have taken seven to ten days to complete on foot.

Needless to say, moving to a new environment can result in anxiety. Having changed locations more times than I can count, I know this to be true. Moving is stressful, but mostly moving is about U-Haul: You hauling stuff you don't need and never use from one place to another.

Moving is also dramatic. My most recent "Now what?" included a transition from an urban neighborhood in the Bay to our new home in the deep woods of the Pacific Northwest. I never dreamed that selling our house in California would be so complicated. Preparing our home built in 1926 to be put on the market became more than a chore. It was a nightmare. After spending days painting our dated yellow kitchen a modern shade of gray, we were horrified to discover the paint drying in uneven shades. We later discovered that the paint was somehow defective, and we ended up starting over and repainting the room—several times!

That was only the beginning of our ordeal. A historic drought of four years came to an end in our part of California just as we scheduled our first open house, bringing a Noah's ark-scale downpour of rain that turned our backyard into a small pond. Our new pond scared away most of the potential buyers—city dwellers not ready to commit to "lakefront" property.

In a red-hot real estate market, only one buyer emerged for our home, but one offer was all we needed. After a lot of packing and unpacking, we arrived in Washington. We found several advantages to this new "Now what?" place. The forest was a perfect setting to recover from our high-stress city life in California. It would be healing and life giving to breathe in the aroma of tall pine trees and watch the deer feed in our new backyard. Perhaps my new environment could become an ideal place to recover from our recent church experience and our noisy, intense city life. My new life in the woods did leave one concern: *where do I go from here?* Moreover, the "Now what?" question touches on a deeper question of the heart: "Who am I?" I left most of my identity in California. My husband was launching his new career as director of a new department at a university, while my previous world was all about church. Most of my energy had been spent on our ministry in our city, working through the logistics of church life, meetings, and preparing sermons. We had also been greatly involved in organizations in our community. I was no longer the pastor of a church or a member of an influential community organization. The "Who am I?" question grew into "Who am I *if*...?" Who am I *if* I am not a pastor, *if* I am no longer part of a church? For others, this question may be, "Who am I *if*" I am not a wife, a teacher, an executive of a company, and so on.

Like Ruth, I wondered how I would go about building a new life. Perhaps Ruth was wondering the same things when she arrived in Bethlehem.

Hope has a beginning. Regardless of the magnitude of the transition, I believe each one offers an opportunity for moving on to the next place. I reassured myself, "Just one step is all you need for now. If you can put one foot forward on your new path, the rest will follow suit. Don't try to figure out the big picture and the complicated universe that makes up for your life; just work on your first move."

When Ruth arrived in Bethlehem with Naomi, she may have wondered what her first move would be. Her reasoning led her to the most logical place: the harvest field. She may have concluded, "Well I'm here, and there's a harvest field nearby; I'll just start there."

With her mother-in-law's permission, Ruth courageously headed to work in a field owned by Naomi's prominent relative, Boaz. Boaz soon noticed her, impressed by her virtuous reputation, and promoted her to glean grain with the women working in his field. When Boaz discovered her loyalty to her mother-in-law, he rewarded Ruth with extra privileges in the form of bread and extra grain.

Like Ruth, I had to find my first step in Washington. Our move brought with it the challenge to find new friends, a church, and some sort of career. I relished the break from the city and the release from the pressures of being a pastor. Yet, like Ruth, I needed to find my first step. I had yet to discover my new harvest field.

My relative Emily found her first step this way:
What helped me to be a part of the community? Old and new friends, hospitality (especially eating around a table with others), accepting help more than just the day of the funeral, LISTENING, LISTENING, LISTENING. Telling my stories and memories about Don.

In the process of establishing my new life, I have had to tell myself that nothing has to be perfect. I need not make the *perfect* decision, find the *perfect* job, or expect the *perfect* life. God is not a game show host who sends us home without a prize if we offer the wrong answer. In my encounters with students at our last church, many struggled because they wanted to do everything perfectly. They feared making mistakes in choosing their classes, majors, or investing in careers they might later regret. I reassured them there are only two things in life you need to get right: your relationship with God and the choice of who to marry. All the rest is mostly a work-around.

Ruth likely was not thinking about her long-term future. She was focusing on the wheat, on her small part, on her little beginning gleaning in the field.

I started my new life by engaging in small, insignificant activities. I planted flowers. Perhaps this was not a huge breakthrough, but adding color in the decorative containers next to the front door seemed like a good beginning. After the flowers, I gathered the courage to attend an evening meeting at a women's conference several miles from my home. I hoped that this could be a start to making new friends. It didn't go well. I bravely began the evening with a long drive to a church thirty miles away. The sun was rapidly setting. I would soon be taking on this challenge in the dark. This was my first time driving a long distance from my home since moving into my new home less than two weeks prior. I didn't even know my way around my neighborhood, much less the county in which I lived. I arrived fifteen minutes late and was greeted by a friendly group of young women who gave me a lanyard. I proceeded to find my way into a sanctuary that felt like a sea of hundreds of strange faces. As soon as I entered the auditorium and heard the worship music, I was overcome with emotion. All the pain I experienced from our ministry in California came rushing over me as though someone was pouring a large bucket of water over my head. It was all I could do to keep from exiting the auditorium and driving home. Instead, I talked myself into staying until the service was over.

My attempt to step out in faith became a disaster. Instead of a nurturing experience at the women's event, I end up crying, getting lost in the pitch dark on the long drive, and encountering a driver with road rage. Nonetheless, the nature of stubborn hope is *taking initiative* even at the risk of getting lost on a dark night in the forest. I had discovered that the first steps in transition often prove challenging, similar to the challenge Ruth faced when she went out to glean wheat in a strange field.

This kind of experience may be exasperating, but it is part of our "normal" when walking through the "Now what?" zone. Ruth's story offers another important survival strategy for undergoing change: following wise advice.

Granted, there are times when even sound advice can seem illogical. What would you do if your mother-in-law told you to go sneak into a total stranger's bedroom in the middle of the night? Yet, this is exactly what Naomi suggested and Ruth did!

For most of the women I know this would be unthinkable, but in ancient culture, it made practical sense. Naomi, also a widow, needed to reclaim the inheritance due her deceased husband. Her plan was to accomplish this through Ruth, by bringing her into a Levirate marriage. Biblical scholars explain that the scenario of the Levirate marriage states, "If one brother died without having a son, the next brother was to take the widow and provide an heir for his dead brother" (referenced in Deut. 25:5-10). The plan proposed that Boaz would become Ruth's husband in order "to perpetuate the name of the dead through his inheritance, that the name of the dead may not be cut off from among his brethren" (Ruth 4:10). This act would preserve both Ruth and Naomi's genetic legacy by providing an ancestral line of offspring that remarkably continued into the Messiah's reign. Therefore, we can learn from Ruth's experience that life transitions call for making small steps and consulting wise counsel. Stubborn hope is all about taking the risks to find it. Ruth's courage demonstrates that thriving in the "Now what?" zone involves taking chances, sometimes even big ones.

By all accounts, Ruth took a huge risk when she pursued Boaz. Imagine sneaking into a strange man's tent and curling up at his feet in the middle of the night. Who does that? Hope is a behavior marked by small steps, wise counsel, and risk-taking. Rather than simply a state of freedom from fear, courage is something you *do*. Ruth may have been frightened out of her mind when she quietly stepped into her destiny by tiptoeing into Boaz's tent in the middle of the night, but she did it anyway. At the crossroads of the "Now what?" place, hope starts with finding that first step. Ruth wisely discerned that big undertakings begin with small footprints. She found the key to flourishing in her new environment. She was unaware of what her future would hold as an outsider in a foreign land, but Ruth didn't need the big picture. She just needed a start.

You do not need a degree in astrophysics to appreciate the universe. You only need to gaze at a twinkling star. The best part of landing in the "Now what?" zone happens when you see God's hand at work as you look back on your life.

Little did Ruth anticipate the implications of her journey. Eventually, she and her husband Boaz would become King David's grandparents and an important link to the chain of generations that led to the Messiah, Jesus. Ruth became part of God's redemptive story about the love that sent His Son into the world to sacrifice His life in order to forever change the eternal destiny of humankind.

Now what?

I look forward to my new surroundings as a place of growth and discovery, where my life can blossom like wildflowers on a sunny field in spring. In this place, hope shows me how my life can be part of God's redemptive story for the world.

It is a wonderful thing to have a forest in my backyard. Just breathing the air and gazing at the tall trees has me in awe of a marvelous God. As authors Alan Nelson and Gene Appel observe, "The only truly safe place to be in the Christian walk is smack-dab in the middle of God's will."[1]

I have experienced a significant breakthrough since my unpleasant journey to the women's retreat where I was at the edge of tears. Now, a year later, I am planning on attending the same retreat, but this time I have been recruited as part of a team to pray with women after the service.

Against all odds, Ruth exercised relentless and stubborn hope, walked courageously into the unknown, and yet flourished. If God can write a beautiful story out of her life, He can do the same for me.

Rachel Nichols, a friend from the church I attend in Seattle, wrote a song entitled "Sanctuary" which brought insight and encouragement into my new journey of hope. As I meditate on the lyrics, I can allow God to touch my heart and create hope in His sanctuary.

Sanctuary

By Rachel Nichols

Come sweet Light of the Morn
Gather up the tattered and torn
And it's broken us down
Our homes have been lost
And our days are dark
Come Sweet Lord of Repair
Mend the hearts laid under despair
Our hands can rebuild
What death cannot kill
Our words give new birth
To a formless earth
Chorus
Build your sanctuary on our dry and barren land
Build your sanctuary on our dry and barren land
And we will fill it with...
Hallelujah

We will sing

(repeat)

Come God of Justice and Peace

Lift oppression and bring relief

Guide the displaced

To a welcomed embrace

Tend to our wounds

Healer, make us new

A Prayer

Jesus, I look to you at the crossroads of my "Now what?" place.

Give me the strength and courage I need to take the first step.

Thank you for bringing me to a place where I can grow and flourish;

a place where I can embrace a deeper relationship with you.

Bring me into your arms and into a deeper understanding of your love.

Thank you for the wonderful story you are writing for me with your hand.

Questions for Reflection

- Read Chapter 1 of the book of Ruth. Have you ever been in a "Now what?" place? What did you see as the "first step" you needed to take? What insights is God giving you at this particular season of your life?

- Read Jeremiah 29:11-14. What words of encouragement is God communicating in these verses about your situation?

3

ANNA

Hope Lives

"And coming in that instant she gave thanks to the Lord,
and spoke of Him to
all those who looked for redemption in Jerusalem" (Luke
2:38 NKJV).

Have you ever experienced an event that changed your
life forever? I remember the first time I opened the red and
white paperback New Testament an usher handed to me in
the lobby at church. Beginning at the Gospel of Matthew, I
felt the red-lettered words of Jesus pierce the center of my
being. I knew in a moment that I would never be the same. It
was as though every molecule that made me human shifted
from darkness to light. This was the pivotal moment in my

life when I knew God was real.

Suddenly I knew that Jesus, the Son of God, loved me and the Bible was the truth. I cannot honestly say I "found" Jesus, but clearly Jesus "found" me. He was waiting for me all along.

The day after I encountered the truth of the Gospel, I woke up a different person. Everything was new. Overnight, my values changed from secular to Biblical; my conscience changed from human to Christian. It was as if aliens from outer space had abducted the "old me" and replaced me with someone I had never met. Although this was only the beginning of the work God planned to do in my life, I was thrilled with my relationship with Jesus.

I could barely take in all the excitement. I was driven by an intense zeal for a deeper relationship with this new divine Person who invaded my world with His presence. It wasn't long before I became a constant annoyance to people around me. I could not resist telling everyone I met, even strangers, how God had transformed me into a new person. This very fire which the Holy Spirit ignited in my heart motivated believers, including women, thousands of years ago.

Several accounts in Scripture feature women who were full of the Holy Spirit and zeal for serving God through the same hope I have experienced. If you are unfamiliar with her, let me introduce you to Anna, a woman who stands out among the many influential women of her time. Anna became a significant prophetic voice in the Jewish community at the dawn of Jesus' earthly life. The Gospel of Luke describes her as a devoted elderly woman who demonstrated *stubborn hope* in giving all of her time and energy to God in the temple, serving Him with continual fasting and relentless prayers.

What was so special about Anna that it inspired Luke to include her in his Gospel? For starters, the name Anna originates from the Hebrew for Hannah, meaning "grace." She also comes from a distinctive gene pool. While we know little of her background, we do know that she was the daughter of a man named Phanuel of the tribe of Asher. Asher was Leah's second son by her maid, Zilpah, and one of the twelve tribes that made up the nation of Israel.

Adding to what made her unique, Anna was a prophetess. In ancient times women often served in key roles as prophets. Among these prophetesses were Miriam, the sister of Aaron and Moses; Deborah, the judge of Israel; and Huldah, who foretold Jerusalem's downfall in King Josiah's reign. Add to this list of women prophets the four daughters of Philip the evangelist mentioned in the book of Acts.

Even more unusual, Anna was eighty-four years old

when we read about her in Luke! Remarkably, she did not let her age get in the way of her ministry of prayer in the temple. According to Anna, there was no such thing as retirement when it came to serving God. Luke describes her constant activity in the sunset of her life:

"Now there was one, Anna, a prophetess, the daughter of Phanuel, of the tribe of Asher. She was of a great age, and had lived with a husband seven years from her virginity; and this woman *was* a widow of about eighty-four years, who did not depart from the temple, but served *God* with fastings and prayers night and day" (Luke 2:36-37).

For Anna, worshipping God went beyond her daily routine and became her lifestyle. It is likely that she lived in the part of the temple known as the Court of the Women, the outer section of the Temple where women were permitted to worship. The Court of the Women was also known as the "middle court." Within this specific area, all Jews, male and female, were permitted. It was the largest of the temple courts and a venue for constant music, dancing, and singing. Doubtless, Anna experienced struggles and trials like everyone else. Life as a widow was often extremely difficult. You may recall the challenges widows faced outlined in the previous chapter. Regardless of her challenges, however, Anna experienced a deep relationship with God and loved to serve him in the temple with all of her heart.

I recall the early years of my "Anna" faith. I looked forward to waking up every day to pray and meditate on Scripture, discovering what treasures God had for me. I remember the sweetness and innocence of the "childlike" faith Jesus talked about. As a new believer it never entered my mind that God would not meet every desire I had in my heart. I clearly had a boatload of problems and issues to work through, but somehow it seemed my faith brought joy and excitement that transcended my struggles.

What happened to this woman, my twenty-something self I once knew? Where is *that* woman who could not wait to get up in the morning to read her Bible and see what God was going to do that day? I call my condition *Zombie Christianity*. Slowly, without realizing it, I evolved into one of the walking dead. You won't be able to find the term "zombie" when you search your Bible. Ironically, the very notion is an oxymoron: How can you be alive in Christ and yet be walking around like a dead person at the same time? Yet, this word accurately describes a way of life that can result from the wear and tear of difficult experiences taking their toll on your heart, draining your spiritual life to a flat line.

Fortunately, Zombie Christians are not totally dead. Unlike the undead in the television show, *The Walking Dead*, who wander around looking for their next meal, there still remains some sign of life in us.[1] Zombie believers usually have a relationship with Jesus, are committed to faith in the Bible as God's Word, and have eternal life with Jesus. A Zombie Christian will even pray and exhibit Christian behaviors like attending church, exercising kindness and compassion, and even reaching out to the marginalized — but inside they *feel* dead. They walk around waiting and hoping for someone or something to help them feel alive.

Zombie Christianity reminds me of the almost-dead church of my childhood. Just for fun, let's start with dead animals. I recall one woman (I will call her Mrs. Torgelson) who was heading toward seventy and was a prominent member. She had short, reddish hair and was always fashionably dressed in a bright colored wool coat and a smart brimless hat. Mrs. Torgelson truly stood out due to the dark brown mink stole she wore around her neck with the head of the skinny little animal still attached. This creature gave me the creeps. I felt like it was staring right at me with its beady little glass eyes.

Our church repeated the same gloom and doom "zombie" service every Sunday. I have seen more joy at funerals. Most of the hymns we sang were in minor keys with grim lyrics that served as a constant reminder of how we had failed God. Hearing phrases like "earth is a desert drear" and "such a worm as I" applied wet blankets to my Sunday church experience.

The highlight of the service was the communion that took place each month. Our church treated communion as the funeral Jesus never got. To a background of sad organ music, the congregation would form a long line shuffling forward to await their turn. Everyone was alive and participating, but we all *felt* dead.

Contrary to my church's "undead" experience, Anna's faith was alive with hope in the coming of the Messiah. She had a deep sense of purpose and understood the significance of her life in the temple. She knew how important her prayers were to God and that one day they would bear fruit.

The question becomes: What was Anna's secret explaining her zeal for God? As I read about her in Luke's Gospel, think about her actions, and listen to her words, I ask "What is she up to that keeps her stubborn hope alive?"

Perhaps the best place to begin is by looking at Anna's life in the temple and asking, "What happens when Anna prays?" Several principles are at play in her story.

First, *Anna established a healthy discipline.* Day after day she kept to the plan. The routine, simply put, was to continue going to the temple. Often we can experience breakthroughs in our challenges by just sticking with it. My husband is a lifetime Pittsburgh Steelers fan. He tells me that their coach, Mike Tomlin, believes that a great deal of success is just the result of "showing up for work." I may not be an expert on football, but the idea makes sense. Stay on the path. If your dream is to graduate from college, go to class no matter what.

In our Bay Area church, I encountered several students who had become quite disheartened over their academic performance. I coached them to take their exams regardless of whether or not they felt they had the confidence to pass. In spite of their struggles with teachers and disappointments with grades, most found the courage to remain in college and even graduate.

Routines, however, can become dull. Take exercising for instance. I find working out about as interesting as watching luggage move on a carousel at the airport. I prefer the Ricky Gervais approach. When asked, "What exercise do you do regularly?" his response was, "I lift weights. Then I put them down again." Overall, like almost anything else, exercise pays off if you stick with it. Staying with a plan keeps you moving forward. In my case, one way to "bring Anna back" means staying the course of a daily discipline of meditating on Scripture to fill my mind with God's thoughts and ideas.

The second principle of Anna's hope: *She was focused.* She concentrated on the task in front of her: prayer. Although Luke does not specifically mention this, one can assume that God had Anna's undivided attention, and vice versa. From what we know, she did not allow distractions to keep her from her purpose of remaining in the temple to pray and fast. I envy people like Anna. Sometimes I have the attention span of a cat on a diet of Red Bull.

My husband Earl is the most focused person I know. He puts every ounce of thought, time, and energy into everything he does regardless of the scale of the endeavor. This is one reason why Earl makes the best-grilled cheese sandwiches on the planet. He uses butter melted in the frying pan in addition to spreading it on the outside of whole wheat bread. He then adds a lot more cheddar cheese than is necessary inside of the sandwich. When he works his magic, the result is a slightly darkened toasty sandwich with hot, melted cheese oozing out of the sides and a cold dill pickle spear as a garnish.

I have discovered managing priorities to be among the most effective tools to maintain focus. On a daily basis, I must consider "What is really important today?" Is the important thing what to have for dinner, or which outfit to wear for the event I'm attending? Although these may be legitimate concerns, they are not the big ones. Once I define what really matters in my day, focus keeps my attention there.

Anna held another secret in her heart keeping her motivated to pray: high expectations. Dead people rarely expect anything. The problem with Zombie Christians is that they have no aspirations. Their only hope is finding someone to infect with their walking dead version of Christianity so they will never be disappointed. They do not take any risks, especially when it comes to God.

Anna was a woman who expected great things from God. She expected that He would be faithful to His promises. Why else would she spend so many years seeking God's face through fasting and prayer?

It amazes me how a person's life can change in just one day or in one moment. Finally, after her long season of seeking God, Anna's expectations in the promise of the Messiah were fulfilled. Luke describes how "in that instant she gave thanks to the Lord" (Luke 2:38). Anna had been serving God, praying for decades, and suddenly she discovered that the Messiah she had been waiting for had arrived. The one of whom the angel announced to Mary, that "He will be great, and will be called the Son of the Highest...and of His Kingdom there will be no end" (Luke 1:33).

Although God can give us breakthroughs over time, He

also can make changes in our lives in an instant. In its original language, the phrase "in that instant" describes "a moment, or divinely preset time period; a limited period to accomplish the Lord's specific purpose."[2]

In addition to giving us the grace to wait, God offers us a realm of immediate individual experiences through His Son Jesus. Anna's experience proves that God can make changes in our lives right now. We can experience an encounter with God in an *instant*. One moment with God can change us forever.

Real hope begins in a relationship with Jesus. He will come and find you wherever you are. God's unquenchable passion for us opens the door to *stubborn hope*, an unstoppable force resulting from an encounter with God.

Jesus is all about expectations, encouraging us to ask, seek, and knock. As a new believer in Christ, I was full of anticipation that God would do something exciting in my life every day. My prayers did not come from a misguided sense of greed, but from a reservoir of relationship with Jesus.

Anna's experience proves that great expectations eventually pay off. After many years of praying and seeking God, her expectations in the promise of the Messiah were fulfilled!

Hope is alive. The greatest principle we can learn from

Anna stems from a life filled with the power of the Holy Spirit. After her years of praying and serving God in the temple, something wonderful happened! The Holy Spirit encountered her with the revelation that God's Son Jesus, the long-awaited Messiah, had finally arrived! Her divine purpose to serve God in the temple with her continual prayers had finally brought fruit—the unveiling of God's promise to His people, the birth of the Messiah. Her stubborn hope was realized.

This Christ child came to give His life for us. God's great love would be revealed through the sacrifice of His only Son on the cross. Through Jesus, we are reconciled to our Creator who transforms us into a new creation. When I feel like a Zombie Christian, I can ask the Holy Spirit to fill me again and again. The Spirit can breathe His life into every dead and dry place in my heart. My desire is to bring Anna's experience into my life by receiving a fresh renewal and a new zeal from the Holy Spirit. I look forward to returning to the childlike faith of my 22-year-old self. My prayer mirrors David's request: "Restore to me the joy of my salvation" (Psalm 51:12).

Together, Anna's Spirit-filled life of discipline, focus, and great expectations can encourage those who feel spiritually dry and need a season of refreshing. When Anna prayed, she exemplified stubborn hope: the relentless expectation that waits for the fulfillment of God's promises. Anna set her sights on what was to come, not on yesterday. What was to come in her life in the temple was the arrival of Jesus as a gift to the world. Anna's life exemplifies what I can become—a person filled with the Spirit, excited about Jesus, and expecting Him to show up everywhere.

A Prayer

Thank you, Lord, for your gift of hope.

Breathe your life through all the dead and tired places in my heart.

Restore to me the childlike faith I once knew, so I can trust you more every day.

Fill my heart with a new zeal, a new excitement,

not only for you but for your plan for my future.

Birth in me new dreams, new visions,

and a new sense of your divine purpose for creating me as your child.

Lead me into a deeper intimate relationship with you

and an experience of your presence in my life.

Fill me overflowing with the joy of your Holy Spirit.

Open my understanding to embrace your immeasurable love for me.

Questions for Reflection

- Read Psalm 51 and Revelation 2:1-7. Describe a time when you felt excited about your relationship with Jesus. Has anything changed? If so, what do you think happened?

- What do you see as the major obstacle in cultivating your relationship with Jesus?

- Name three character traits found in Anna that fed her zeal for God. What insights can you apply from her example?

- Read Ephesians 3:14-21. What insight does Paul provide about specific ways you can pray to feel closer to God?

4

SARAH

Hope Laughs

"Is anything too hard for the Lord?" (Genesis 18:14 NKJV)

At around midnight, while I was riveted by the television watching a CNN documentary, it happened. My husband and I were resting comfortably on a king sized bed in a hotel suite when we heard a high-pitched sound pierce the quiet, followed by a soft, intermittent buzzing that seemed to be right within our room.

Earl darted out into the hallway to locate the source of the noise. You guessed it. It was the hotel fire alarm. I panicked. My immediate thought was, "Oh no! We're trapped on the top of the building, and the elevators are shut down! What was I thinking when I booked the tenth floor?"

Frantic, I made myself presentable and dashed out into

the hallway where I found Earl and others leaning over the balcony, staring at the atrium on the ground floor below. The hotel guests looked like helpless passengers at the rail of a burning cruise ship, hoping all is well but edging toward the lifeboats just in case. Needless to say, everyone in the hotel took the warning seriously. No one was thinking, *Let's just go back to sleep. I'm sure it's nothing.*

Fortunately, we didn't see any smoke or indication of a fire, and we had the comfort of watching the fire marshal, who didn't seem in a panic, roam the building.

We all felt great relief when they informed us officially that we were safe. The source of the alarm was an eight-year-old boy stuck in an elevator. His father, in a panic, pulled the fire alarm to get help. The child was soon set free, but the other guests were shocked.

Fire alarms get my attention. Indications of something dangerous or life-threatening cause me to take notice. A buzzing sound in a hotel room is a clue that something is wrong.

On the flip side, I wonder if I would react to good news with that same readiness and vigilance. For example, let's suppose a different type of alarm existed, engineered to sound *only* in the event of good news. This alarm would go off the second medical research discovered a cure for cancer, or the government was about to issue every citizen a tax refund because the federal budget had too much of a surplus. (That will never happen.)

The sound of the "good news alarm" would be unlike the screeching noise of a smoke detector with low batteries. Instead of a deafening and piercing blast, this "alarm" would play upbeat music — perhaps a pop hit, some classical song, a jazz piece, or any tune that felt positive or joyful.

Of course, both good news and bad instantly can be recycled on the Internet. Why does bad news sound so loud and good news seem so quiet? And why is so much of my energy wasted on remaining alert for something bad to happen? Some people may feel it is simply too risky to relax and enjoy life because something might go wrong!

However, in the background, God may be trying to draw my attention to something amazing He is about to do. Would I even believe Him? In fact, God is sending us His good news all of the time. David responds to God's positive initiative with a prayer in the Psalms: "Cause me to hear Your loving kindness in the morning" (Psalm 143:8).

Dwelling on the mental "fire alarms" in life is nothing new. Numerous stories are scattered throughout Scripture of individuals to whom God announced that good news was on the way. Unfortunately, some did not believe Him, at least at first. The Bible is alive with the stories of individuals who struggled to believe God's promises, and yet somehow overcame their doubts in the most difficult situations. Many of those people were women, like Sarah.

You may be familiar with the story of Sarah and Abraham in the Old Testament. God planned to give them a child even in their ripe old age. However, Sarah neglected to pay attention to the "good news alarm" God sent her way. She thought, *Pregnant, at my age? You have got to be kidding!* To her, the idea of experiencing motherhood as a senior citizen was as likely as a flock of sheep flying in a V formation in the sky. And yet, at this late stage of her life, God was trying to turn Sarah's attention to His loving kindness, which He was sending her way. Sarah was unaware of the wonderful surprise God had in store for her.

The story is set thousands of years ago with the elderly couple living a quiet life in a place called Canaan. Abraham is resting by the door of their tent near a grove of Terebinth (oak) trees. In a modern analogy, a retired Abraham is relaxing on a lawn chair, enjoying a cup of coffee next to his luxury motor home at an RV park in the middle of the Arizona desert.

As the story unfolds, Abraham and Sarah are about to be visited by three strangers. Sitting by the tent, Abraham suddenly notices three men standing next to him, and he begins to realize there is something special about these guests.

According to Scripture, these divine visitors represented the Lord and two angels. This is one of many examples in the biblical text of what scholars call a theophany, or a visible appearance of God in human form.

Immediately, Abraham rolls out the red carpet for his distinguished guests and begs them to stay. For Abraham and Sarah, this was typical Bedouin hospitality — nothing was too good for a guest. In that nomadic lifestyle, everyone was welcome, even strangers.

Abraham's open door policy resembles that of my home while growing up in Wisconsin. My mother would serve coffee and snacks to the women in the neighborhood who popped in to sit and chat around our oval oak dining room table.

They came for a variety of purposes. Friends and neighbors would spontaneously drop in to chat, borrow something, or bring us vegetables from their gardens. Mrs. Besau, a graying regular who wore fire engine red lipstick, lived across the street and came over to enjoy her afternoon cigarette. Mrs. Cole lived next door and was particularly fond of our dog Ginger, so she visited primarily to bring her treats. She would enter the house announcing, "I came to see the dog!"

Although our friends and neighbors each possessed their own particular quirks and personalities, our neighborhood guests were no match for Abraham's extraordinary *heavenly* visitors. Abraham immediately recognizes their divine uniqueness and treats them like royalty. He washes their feet, and Sarah quickly bakes bread. Abraham rushes out to his herd, selects his best calf, and gives it to his servant to prepare. He "wines and dines" the guests. And he stands by his guests as they eat in accordance with another Bedouin custom expected of hosts.

It isn't long before the divine guests have a question for Abraham, but the question is not about him! They ask, "Where is Sarah, your wife?" Although the Lord had previously paid a special visit to Abraham to announce His promise of their future son, this visit was about Sarah. She was about to hear the miraculous news that soon she would become a mother! The divine messengers announce to Abraham: "Sarah your wife shall have a son" (Genesis 18:10).

Meanwhile, from inside the tent, Sarah can hear Abraham's conversation with the guests. Bedouin custom forbade women eating meat with men, especially strangers. The mysterious visitors now have Sarah's undivided attention. As she listens in on the discussion between her husband and the strange visitors about the future birth of their child, she must be thinking: *Are you insane? I'm 90 years old!* Unsurprisingly, Sarah does not take the visitor's news seriously.

After so many years of disappointment due to being childless, Sarah fails at that moment to recognize divine news from heaven. Consequently, Sarah does what would come natural for any woman in her situation: She laughs.

Sarah's laughter is not one of happiness over the news of a miracle child in their future. She isn't thinking, *I'm finally going to become a mother! Wait till Hagar hears about this!* (Hagar being the maid Sarah loaned to Abraham as her surrogate who successfully gave birth to a son.) Instead, she chuckles in disbelief, "After I have grown old, shall I have pleasure, my lord being old also?" (Genesis 18:12)

Both Abraham and Sarah are far beyond the age of childbearing. In fact, they are past the age of doing most everything. She may be wondering how they are going to "make it happen" with a 99-year-old husband who is, as the writer of Hebrews describes, "as good as dead" (Hebrews 11:12).

Unfortunately, the heavenly visitors do not share her sense of humor. They make no attempt to validate her feelings with reflective listening skills, nor is their response like that of a trained counselor who might say: "Talk to me about your laugh. I understand given the circumstances how difficult this must be for you to believe." On the contrary, the angels seem puzzled and wonder aloud: "Why did Sarah laugh, saying, 'Shall I surely bear a *child*, since I am old?' Is anything too hard for the Lord?" (Genesis 18:13-14).

When she denies it, they confront her: "No, you did laugh!" Then again, let's give Sarah a break. Imagine what she had to endure for those 90 years of her life. First, she had to leave the comforts of home to embark on a fifteen hundred mile camping trip in the desert (from Ur to Haran to Canaan) with all of their belongings. Imagine preparing for an expedition of this magnitude in an age without downsizing, garage sales, and moving companies. Moreover, she was destined for a long trip with a 75-year-old man who, according to the book of Hebrews, "went out, not knowing where he was going" (11:8).

Making matters worse, Abraham, in order to save his own life, attempted to "traffic" Sarah twice on their journey to two different kings. On top of this humiliating treatment, Sarah faced the challenge of infertility all of her life, adding to the long list of her misfortunes.

The long road of lingering disappointment usually leads to frustration. When I am discouraged, I become frustrated over insignificant problems like losing my phone or car keys, or experiencing our Internet functioning at a snail's pace. If I see one more of those tiny multi-colored wheels spinning around on my laptop screen, I am going to throw my computer out the back door!

My trivial issues are nothing compared to communities who suffer through monumental struggles, like desperate refugees from all parts of the world who are forced to leave their homes and settle in the safety net of foreign nations. Many individuals from fractured people groups would doubtless give anything for the luxury of pampered American problems. However, my deep concern for the plight of displaced people groups does not make my own frustrations disappear.

The partner of discouragement is the feeling of failure. I faced this experience often in the church we started in California, as I described in my journal at the time:

The thing about failure, especially a significant disappointment, is that it takes on a life of its own. It finds a way to spread like a virus into other areas of your life. It's almost like an email has been sent out: "Cross these people off your list!" People can smell failure, especially in churches. And when they smell it, they flee. Who wants to be around a failure?

For Sarah, it is likely she faced not only personal feelings of failure, but a sense of having failed to measure up to her society's standards for women. In ancient culture, having children was an expectation. Hebrew women were trained from childhood by their older female relatives to cook, sew, and tend children in preparation for the honored position of motherhood. Women's social position and sense of personal fulfillment depended on success in that role.

To add insult to injury, Sarah knew that most couples desired to have children, and they considered them a status symbol. Married couples without children were treated with pity and sometimes even suspicion. Why had God not blessed them with offspring? Infertility was assumed to be the woman's fault, so many looked on barren women as incomplete and somehow out of God's favor.

Finally, after years of despair, Sarah gives up on her dream of motherhood and offers her personal assistant Hagar to Abraham as a surrogate wife. This custom was not unusual at the time. One commentator writes, "In the legal custom of that day, a barren woman could give her maid to her husband as a wife, and the child born of that union was regarded as the first wife's child. The husband then could adopt her son and the son would be the official heir."[1]

Compounding Sarah's suffering, her maid becomes pregnant and treats her with contempt. Co-wives commonly taunted childless women in this time. Sometimes the people you know can be the greatest sources of discouragement. As a child, I frequently struggled with low self-esteem. At this fragile stage in my life when I needed love and affirmation, I instead became a victim of constant bullying by classmates and teachers. At my high school, those who failed to conform to unspoken standards became targets for abuse. The criteria for girls mandated that we be pretty, popular, smart, or athletic to be accepted. If nothing else, a wealthy background or a father who was a business executive would do. Those who failed to fit into at least one of these pigeonholes could count on being ostracized by the other students. Unfortunately, according to my peers I fell short in every area, making me a victim of endless verbal cruelty from some of my classmates. I found no escape from the constant taunting of my peers.

Walking home from school one day at about age six, I was ambushed by a boy a few years older than me (I will call him "Jim") who lived in my neighborhood. Joined by his friend who lived down the street, Jim punched me in the mouth while his friend held me down.

Bullying has side effects that go beyond intimidation for the victim. These experiences limit our senses of self-worth, confidence, and courage to pursue or even have goals for one's life.

Imagine the negative effects Sarah experienced due to bullying in her ancient culture. Coupled with decades of disappointment from infertility and Hagar's smug attitude. Sarah finally "settled" and resorted to sarcasm as a way of life.

Sarah's unbelieving laughter is similar to some forms of cynicism that have crept into our society. She represents countless individuals who have become jaded toward God. I have met people who fall into this category whose hearts have turned cold as a result of negative experiences and unhealthy examples of "Christianity" they have seen. In fact, I have noticed that cynicism has even becoming stylish in some areas of the world. It seems as though people admire those who are negative, jaded, self-righteous, or critical. Sarcasm toward others, life, and God makes certain individuals appear intellectual and well-informed. These people believe that they "get it" and happy people do not. Although the cynical Sarahs of the world do not speak for everyone, life sometimes beats us all up like classmate bullies. The fallback position is to crawl, with Sarah, into a safe hole of unbelief.

Can God give hope to those who have given up? This is the question of Sarah's life. Let's start by diving deeper into her story. In spite of what her circumstances indicate, Sarah's life wasn't over. On the contrary; it was just beginning! Similarly, if you have been disillusioned because of your circumstances, your story is not over yet. God has a different plan for all the Sarahs who feel God has given up on them, or worse, those who believe He does not even exist.

Something wonderful happened that changed the course of Sarah's life forever! God's miraculous event transformed not only her life, but the eternal future of generations to come who would find redemption through the seed of Abraham, God's Son Jesus.

A spirit of skepticism blinds us to the sovereign work of the Holy Spirit. At each discouraging juncture of Sarah's life, God was working His redemptive story into her future. She was unaware that God had profound things in store for her even beyond having a child. He had a bigger picture in mind. One day, their ancestral line would include the savior of humankind who would change the world!

Years earlier, God had promised Abraham that he would make him a great nation: "I will bless you and make your name great ... And in you all the families of the earth shall be blessed" (Genesis 12:2-3). He had destined Abraham to become the father of many nations: "No longer shall your name be called Abram, but your name shall be Abraham; for I have made you a father of many nations" (17:5).

These were Sarah's promises too! God had a plan to change Sarai's name to Sarah (from "princess" to "The Princess"). Kings of peoples would arise from her descendants and would bring about God's redemptive plan through Jesus.

Deep in the mysteries of hope, God is doing hidden

works in unseen areas of your life. In his letter to the Romans, Paul writes, "hope that is seen is not hope; for why does one still hope for what he sees? But if we hope for what we do not see, we eagerly wait for *it* with perseverance" (Romans 8:24-25).

Fortunately, our doubts do not disqualify us from receiving God's promises. Sarah's new faith was born from her depths of discouragement. Sarah's life reveals the paradox of hope: God will grant faith to those who need it the most, not to those who "deserve" it.

Remarkably, Sarah's doubts and cynicism did not prevent God's power from invading her life. God's great love and grace far outweigh our unbelief. Sarah's story reveals how heartaches cannot isolate us from God. Regardless of where we are, God finds us. He found Sarah in the midst of deep disappointment in the middle of the desert.

Hope has a voice. It calls us to look beyond our circumstances. God challenged Abraham to count the stars: "Look now toward heaven, and count the stars if you are able to number them...So shall your descendants be" (Genesis 15:5). This promise would be fulfilled through both Abraham and Sarah. Ultimately, the stars dotting the evening sky would become her own descendants. Jesus was destined to come from this couple's designated ancestral line. Christ would become the true "seed" of Abraham (Galatians 3:16) through his sacrificial death on the cross.

Overall, human failures cannot determine God's destiny for our lives. It's how the story ends that counts. Notice the happy ending of Sarah's rugged journey: "And the Lord visited Sarah as He said, and the Lord did for Sarah as He had spoken. For Sarah conceived and bore Abraham a son in his old age, at the set time of which God had spoken to him" (Genesis 21:1-2). Regardless of Sarah's despair, God's stubborn hope saw her through to her miracle.

God names her son Isaac, meaning "he laughs," as a reminder of the new joyful laughter God gave to both Sarah and Abraham. Imagine Sarah as she cradles her infant tenderly in her arms. In Sarah's words, you can almost visualize a fountain of joy springing from a heart that was once dead: "'God has made me laugh, *and* all who hear will laugh with me' She also said, 'Who would have said that Sarah would nurse children? For I have borne *him* a son in his old age" (Genesis 21:6-7). God gives Sarah a new laugh. Her once sarcastic demeanor turns to a laughter of joy.

Throughout our ministry, I have met countless discouraged individuals who could use a new laugh. Many of these people are casualties of circumstances that have caused their hearts to grow frail and despondent, trapped in addiction, facing tragic loss, or finding themselves in situations over which they have no control.

Research indicates several health benefits of a sense of humor. Laughter boosts the immune system, burns calories, lowers stress hormones, relaxes your muscles, and decreases pain to name a few. Laughter really is the best medicine.

If human laughter can be so life-giving, imagine how powerful the laughter God gives can be. No individual is too deep in despair that God cannot reach them with a newfound joy for life.

Hope laughs. In my search for hope, my prayer is that God would give me the laugh He gave Sarah. The laugh He desires for us is separate from our circumstances. It's a joy that can only come from the Holy Spirit in the midst of trials. In the Scriptures, Nehemiah's' encouraging words remind us, "the joy of the Lord is your strength" (Nehemiah 8:10).

Sarah's sarcastic laugh turned into an "Isaac laugh" because Isaac had come into her world. Like Sarah, God wants to change your laugh from the smirk of cynicism to an expression of joy — a laugh suddenly erupting in the surprise breakthrough you never thought possible.

The new laugh God has for us requires our belief that God is in the miracle business. The angelic beings of Genesis 18 declared to Abraham, "Is anything too hard for the Lord?" God has so much for us to look forward to, including more laughter. If a 90-year-old woman can have a baby, imagine what God can do in your life.

A Prayer

Dear Lord Jesus, thank you for helping me realize

how much you are aware of my disappointments.

Right now, I'm giving all of my frustrations, my doubts, and

my places of despair to you,

placing them in your hands.

Help me to learn how to listen to your encouraging voice

and to

the good news you have waiting for me concerning my

circumstances.

Thank you for all of the miracles you have in store for me.

Turn my laughter of cynicism to a new laughter of joy

over your marvelous work in my life.

Questions for Reflection

- What are specific areas in your life where you could
  use a new laugh?

- Read I Corinthians 2:9-10, Ephesians 3:14-21 and
  Romans 8:18-39. What good news does God have for
  you to which He is drawing your attention?

- Read Psalm 37:1-6. What is the greatest desire of
  your heart? What insight about prayer does David
  reveal in this section of scripture?

5

MARY

Hope Sings

"For He who is mighty has done great things for me, And
holy *is* His name"
(Luke 1:49 NKJV).

I learned early in life never to complain around my
mother. Regardless of my problem, with the exception of
serious illness or injury, her answer was simple and
predictable: "You should be grateful!" She was constantly
reminding me that *some* people are deprived of many
advantages I took for granted. For instance, on the rare
occasion when my siblings and I didn't appreciate her choice
of food for the dinner table (liver and onions for example)
she would scold, "*Some* people don't have anything to eat."
At that time, it was people starving in China. If I grumbled
about not having the latest "in" thing that all the girls were

wearing, her answer was, "You should be grateful. Your dad works hard to put food on the table, *some* people…" "*Some* people" didn't have clothes to wear, didn't have homes, didn't have parents, and so on. I knew if I complained about a headache she might say, "You should be grateful! Some people don't have heads!"

My mom's "Always be thankful because others have it worse than you" ideology made little sense to me. Why be grateful for annoyances like the wood ticks I would discover on my legs from playing outdoors, or the freezing weather I grew up with in Wisconsin, or the math homework that plagued me? For that matter, why would I appreciate simple annoyances like creamed corn? I detested creamed corn. By the time I reached adulthood, I found the principle of gratitude not only difficult, but at times irritating.

As I reflect back on my life, I realize that in some strange way and as much as I hate to admit it, my mother was right. Like all parents, she was imperfect. Empathy and listening may not have been her greatest strengths. Nonetheless, I discovered she was onto a vitally important ingredient for emotional and spiritual health.

Unfortunately, wisdom that is true in theory often can seem impossible in practice. Though I find it easy to express gratitude to people, thanking God doesn't come naturally to me. For example, my first thought when I wake up in the morning is *coffee*. After my caffeine fix, perhaps I can entertain more spiritual thoughts. There are also distractions we all face in our personal struggles that consume the attention we could devote to worshipping God.

I find it reassuring that God does not require me to *feel* thankful simply for the mere privilege of being alive. Authentic gratitude is demonstrated by behavior. A truly thankful and obedient person believes that God deserves worship regardless of how he or she feels in a given moment.

Seeds of gratitude blossom into a healing tool in your life. A thankful spirit works as an effective antidote to despair, similar to the release of endorphins though exercise. God is not interested in our thanking Him out of obligation, religious duty, or fear. Instead, God wants us to thank Him for the simple reason that He is good. Furthermore, when we show our praise to God, we place our lives in the center of His will. As the Apostle Paul declares, "in everything give thanks; for this is the will of God in Christ Jesus for you" (1 Thessalonians 5:18).

In essence, gratitude is a decision. Recently, country singer Carrie Underwood was recovering from several injuries sustained during a fall on the front steps of her home, including a broken wrist and several stitches on her face. Her reaction included these words: "I honestly don't know how things are going to end up but I know this: I am grateful ... that it wasn't much, much worse. And I am grateful for the people in my life that have been there every step of the way."[1]

I believe my search for hope begins with this premise: allowing my soul to express gratitude to God for who He is and what He has done for me. If I look closely enough, I can locate points of gratitude to occupy my day and make worship a lifestyle instead of an event.

The challenge becomes assimilating this powerful tool into my daily life. How do I shift my focus from my personal concerns to give honor to God for all of His majesty and greatness?

Although gratitude comes in many forms, one of the most common means found in the Scriptures is poetry and song.

Hope has a song. Music filled my early years. Together with my two sisters, we harmonized to the latest tunes on the AM radio while washing the dinner dishes. My family would burst into a cappella singing during long road trips in the car to relieve the boredom. I am not convinced that James Corden actually started the popular "carpool karaoke" trend! Something happens when people sing, even if they are not a celebrity riding with a talk show host.

Stubborn hope, a relentless aspiration that surfaces against all odds, begins with gratitude. The Scriptures are alive with songs, hymns, and testimonies from individuals who expressed their praises to God for His marvelous deeds on their behalf. Moreover, the hope of the Gospel message—Jesus' death and resurrection—cannot be contained in preaching and teaching alone. For this reason, Christian churches throughout the world devote a special time in their services to worship. Hope needs to sing.

People of my generation are usually the only ones to recall the late Cliff Barrows, the soloist known for his hymn performances at Billy Graham crusades. Barrows described Christianity as a "singing faith." He believed that "Christian faith is a singing faith, and a good way to express it and share it with others is in community singing."[2] The idea of singing faith, however, extends beyond directing choirs or singing Christian hymns.

I met my husband while participating in a faith-based singing group in my early twenties. We toured throughout the Midwest and East Coast in a dark green van we called "Moby Pickle" performing Christian concerts. I sang and I had faith, but I am not sure my faith was "singing." In practical terms then, the question becomes, what does "singing faith" look like?

Using the common cliché, singing faith can be described as an *attitude of gratitude* to God for who He is. Gratitude begins with discovering that special song inside of us hiding beneath our problems, distractions, and wounds.

I was inspired recently by the Dominican Sisters of Mary from Ann Arbor, Michigan who made the Top Billboard Classical and Holiday Charts with their recent album *Jesu, Joy of Man's Desiring: Christmas with the Dominican Sisters of Mary*. The sisters maintain they are just praying on their albums. As they pray and sing every day, their prayers transform into songs of worship to Christ.

In essence, when we have reached the limit of our faith, there is a song or story of gratitude and hope inside of us waiting to be written.

Somewhere deep in the heart of every person, a song or form of self-expression is waiting for release. Whether your song is in the form of music, journaling, prayer, poetry, or other means, songs are an effective tool for self-expression. In the Old Testament, David released deep, personal songs from within as poured out his heart in the form of intimate prayers to God.

The main focus of this chapter is to challenge us (myself included) to create our own special sonnets of poetry written exclusively to Jesus. Songs of gratitude to God need not be eloquent or even set to music. We need not possess musical talent like Taylor Swift or Billy Joel to write our own song. Our "song" includes simply those words that come from our heart, as we allow the power of the Holy Spirit to write through us. Your song will express your personality and may come in a variety of forms—perhaps as poetry, essay, or work of art.

The female songwriters of the Bible are a valuable source of insight on creating your own song. Mary, the mother of Jesus, pens one of the most inspiring poetic works of worship to God found in the Bible. Mary is a classic example of a person who exemplified "singing faith" as a lifestyle. Among the most grateful individuals in the New Testament, Mary was overcome with praise to God for His mighty works in her life following the angel's announcement that she would become the mother of the Son of God. Out of her deep gratitude, a powerful song emerged.

Traditionally known as "The Magnificat," the song of Mary found in the Gospel of Luke (1:46-55) has become one of the great hymns of the Church. Her song, a prophetic work through the power of the Holy Spirit, tells a remarkable story of the works God performed in her life and the character of the One who she calls, "God my Savior" in Luke 1:47.

Mary was so overcome with gratitude that she could not contain her joy—so much so that she poured out her heart in a divinely inspired poem that has become one of the most familiar Scripture songs commemorating Christ's birth.

Mary's amazing song contains the keys to singing faith.

How do I compose a personal song of gratitude, especially when it seems like nothing is going the way I'd like? How do I sing when I am treated rudely at work, or my doctor affirms I need surgery? When my car needs a new transmission the same week I have to pay my rent, or I am just trying to make it through the day?

Many modern songwriters have specific strategies. For example, Taylor Swift began writing songs in childhood. She has a wide audience, many of whom are teenage girls who can identify with her songs about life and love.

Here's how Swift describes her songwriting strategy:

My first thing when I write song is that I transport myself into my memory land. Then I'll start to find something that I've never told anyone about it. I'm a very quiet person as in I keep everything to myself. It's hard sometimes. But I find it's my only way to build a wall against people who have the intention of hurting me.

The next thing I would do is to try and capture that scene or that certain emotion. Slowly, you'll feel that emotion or scene ... sort of happening in you again. It makes you feel like you're back in the past and feel everything that you had once felt.

Next thing I would do is that after that movie flashing back thing happened, I kinda have that brainstorming of phrases, words…It's like writing story but instead of writing a long story, you can write a short story about that scene or emotion that you had captured just now. (I always carry around my diary, my phone, pen, headphone. Sometimes when I'm doing something suddenly I have this flash back or a phrase. Then I'll quickly write it down or take note on my phone.) By doing this step, you can actually write a lot of different type of verses for all kinds of songs that you want to write.[3]

Of course, I'm not comparing the mother of Jesus with a pop culture celebrity. While Taylor Swift finds inspiration in her experiences, Mary produces a prophetic oracle out of God's promise; words that would endure through the ages. The good news is, like Mary, you do not need a strategy to compose your song. As mentioned earlier, you need not put songs of gratitude to music. Remember Luke's remark that Mary *said* these words. There is no evidence she actually sang them or was musically gifted.

Mary's work illustrates the most important feature of a singing faith: a belief that expresses gratitude to the God who gives hope. Her poem serves as an example of how the Holy Spirit can create canticles of praise in the hearts of ordinary people. The lyrics of her famous song serve as a source of inspiration for anyone desiring to learn about the essence of singing faith. Allow your heart to follow her joyful song as it captures what God has done for her.

First, a personal song flows out of passionate emotions and personal experiences. Mary's song opens with: "My soul magnifies the Lord, And my spirit has rejoiced in God my Savior" (Luke 1:46-47). These words flow from the depths of her being and express the content of her soul and her spirit. The context of "soul and spirit" refers to the seat of affections and will: a person's distinct identity or individual personality. Every facet of her character and the DNA of who she is rejoices and magnifies God. As one of the psalmists writes, "I will sing to the Lord as long as I live; I will sing praise to my God while I have my being" (Psalm 104:33).

Next, I can sing about the great things God has done in my life. Mary's poem centers on the greatness of God! She sings, "For He who is mighty has done great things for me" (Luke 1:49). Her faith rests in how great God is! Imagine being chosen as the mother of Jesus! "For He has regarded the lowly state of His maidservant," she declares. "For behold, henceforth all generations will call me blessed" (1:48).

Out of all of the godly Jewish women in the land of

Israel, why did God select such a humble girl as Mary? An unknown village woman living in a small town of little significance and likely a teenager, Mary found favor in the eyes of a God who had a specific destiny for her life.

A singing faith tells a personal story about God's hand in the lives of people who put their trust in Him. God can reach down to wherever we are and raise us up to the person He has called us to become. David writes about God as the great equalizer in Psalm 138:6, stating, "Though the Lord *is* on high, Yet He regards the lowly; But the proud He knows from afar." God is not partial. Even though Mary was special, highly favored, and the mother of Jesus, she was a person just like us! God desires to lift us up from where we are.

Mary stands as an example, particularly to teenage girls, to never underestimate God's plan for your life or His intention to use you in a powerful way. There is only one mother of Jesus, but there are Marys everywhere — women in whom God wants to do great things. To the Mary I encountered last week while she was sweeping the tile floor of a fast food restaurant and struggling to speak English, I say, "You are the favored one!"

A singing faith also finds inspiration in distress and heartbreaks. This happens when I choose to worship God in the secret places of my heart through both happy times and difficult seasons in my life. We can sing through our heartbreaks as well as our joys. Your song can include the personal battles you have both faced and overcome. Write about them. Record your thoughts and feelings about your situation. See if in the midst of it all, an ember of hope begins to burn from the heart you thought had died.

Mary faced her own challenges. Upon hearing the news that she was with child, Joseph was about to divorce her. Imagine her friends and neighbors' skepticism toward a woman claiming to be the epic definition of an oxymoron: a pregnant virgin.

Some of the best lyrics can come from feeling discouraged or disappointed. During these times, one can discover hope hidden in the form of self-expression. Wherever life finds you, write your song. The psalmist David was inspired not only by God's greatness, but by bouts of discouragement. Often David found comfort in expressing his distress through his prayers. Many of his psalms reveal the sad notes of despondency that often plagued his life: "Why do You stand afar off, O Lord? *Why* do You hide in times of trouble?" (Psalm 10:1).

Some of the most poignant and powerful hymns throughout history were written out of despair. One hymn in particular comes to mind. The composer Horatio Spafford penned "It is Well with My Soul" in the late nineteenth century as a response to the tragic shipwreck that took the lives of his four children.

The reality for most people, including myself, is that we do not feel like bursting into song in the middle of a committee meeting, like a cast member of a Broadway musical announcing to the audience, "I feel a song coming on! Let's just sing our cares away!" However, there is a method to this madness. I can express appreciation for the times God has worked in significant areas of my life. I can begin my prayers by thanking God for the little things I would normally take for granted, like the gift of another day.

Finally, your song can express a new faith in God's miracles. A singing faith is based on trusting God for what seems impossible. As the Apostle Paul explained, "For we were saved in this hope, but hope that is seen is not hope; for why does one hope for what he sees?" (Romans 8:24). Hope entails a new way of seeing, giving us eyes to see the impossible coming to fruition.

Mary had only one practical concern regarding the angel Gabriel's announcement: "How can this be, since I do not know a man?" (Luke 1:34). Mary's question reflects the faith concerns of many people still wondering, *How can this be?* How can I get married when I have yet to meet anyone who could be a potential spouse? How can I pay my rent when I am still looking for a job? How can I make it into a graduate school when I am competing with so many other applicants?

Whoever heard of a virgin birth? Mary didn't depend on her own strength to make this first-time miraculous phenomenon happen. Mary's song brings hope to all those asking their own personal *How can this be?* questions. Her composition overflows with praises to the Lord for everything He is and for all He does.

Mary's song was dedicated to the God who had "shown strength with His arm;...scattered *the* proud in the imagination of their hearts...put down the mighty from *their* thrones, And exalted the lowly...[and] filled *the* hungry with good things" (Luke 1:51-53). Her inspirational composition reflected on all of God's wonderful deeds involved in giving birth to His son. It reveals that gratefulness is the gateway to having hope. Mary discovered God's stubborn hope in His never giving up on the human race by sending His Son into the world.

Perhaps it is time to write your new song.

Thanking God with our songs, even when we don't feel like it, gives us access to His vision for our lives. He desires that we discover hope not only in our circumstances but in trusting in who He is. Mary's song provides an example of what happens when we give God access to the creative talents we use to express ourselves. When we sing out of hope, we experience a form of release that lifts our hearts.

Mary will forever be revered, not only as the mother of Jesus, but also for her faith in a God who performs miracles! She relied on God for her ability to hope. She believed in the angel's words, "with God nothing will be impossible" (Luke 1:37).

Mary believed that God was great in both her personal life and in the world throughout generations. Like Mary, regardless of what you are facing today, He can create a new song out of your life—a song about His power, His love, and His miracles. God is still in the songwriting business. There is a song waiting to rise up in you right now!

Mary's song brings to mind the new songs God has for us—songs about God's greatness and love. Like Mary, David also found his new song:

"He also brought me up out of a horrible pit,

Out of the miry clay,

And set my feet upon a rock,

And established my steps.

He has put a new song in my mouth—

Praise to our God;

Many will see *it* and fear,

And will trust in the Lord." (Psalm 40:2-3)

It's time to sing.

A Prayer

Thank you, Father, for the new song you have placed inside
my heart.

Help me to express my thoughts, fears, hopes,

and especially my gratitude for all you have done in my life.

Let my song be an expression of your deep love for me.

Create in me a grateful heart.

Let my gratitude for who you are become more than a
decision, but a lifestyle,

and help me to recognize your goodness in my
circumstances.

Open my eyes to the wonderful works you are doing in my
life.

Questions for Reflection

- Name at least five blessings from God that you are
  thankful for.

- Read Psalm 136, Ephesians 5:15-21, and 1
  Thessalonians 5:28. What steps can you take to
  integrate gratitude in your life? What are some
  practical ways to assimilate a spirit of gratitude into
  your life?

- Read Psalm 40:1-5 and 144:9-10. What thoughts or feelings do you want your new song to express to God?

6

A WOMAN OUT OF OPTIONS

Hope Thinks

"When she heard about Jesus, she came behind *Him* in the crowd and touched His garment. For she said, 'If only I may touch His clothes, I shall be made well'" (Mark 5:27-28 NKJV).

While rummaging through my purse to grab my driver's license, it hit me. In the frantic rush to leave the house, the emotional fog of my mother's recent death enveloping me, I had left my wallet at home along with my common sense. My last-minute decision to change handbags before I left for the airport had meant transferring my belongings from one purse to another. Somehow my wallet, along with my driver's license, did not make the trip and were lying on the dining room table.

We had just arrived at the Oakland International terminal and were about to get in line for the security checkpoint to board our flight to Milwaukee, Wisconsin for the funeral. My mother had passed away quietly at the age of ninety-one from a brain aneurism.

What was I thinking when I changed handbags? Why do I need to carry a ton of stuff everywhere I go, forcing me to replace my small purse with a larger one? Surely, I could have found enough space in the handbag I originally planned to use, but there was no time for regrets. This was an emergency, and I needed to come up with a solution *fast*. I panicked. Earl and I frantically discussed my options, amounting to zero. A 25-mile round trip to our house and back to retrieve my wallet would mean missing the flight. We had no way of knowing if flights later in the day had available seats. Moreover, delaying my flight another day left much less time to be with my family.

To put it bluntly: I was out of ideas. There I was, at the airport, boarding pass in hand. I was even pulling the official black carry-on roller bag of American air travel. Everything had checked out except for one thing: without a driver's license I would not be boarding my flight.

Running out of ideas is common to all. Finding proven

solutions—not so much. Nonetheless, there are countless stories in Scripture devoted to individuals who overcame daunting1 challenges, and these stories endure as a constant source of inspiration.

One of my very favorite biblical narratives features a courageous woman who was by all accounts *out of ideas*. You may be familiar with her story in the Gospels. This unnamed woman suffered from a chronic hemorrhaging condition, yet she was determined to reach out and grab hold of Jesus' clothing as he passed through her village.

My initial mental image of her suggests an older, gaunt, and shabbily-dressed woman bent over from crippling arthritis. However, this may not have been the case. Biblical scholars note that her symptoms may have resulted from a menstrual disorder or uterine hemorrhage, meaning she could have been in her twenties, as these conditions sometimes began in puberty.

Given that life spans at that time were about 40 years, and we know that her condition had persisted for a period of twelve years, we can conclude that she may have been a young woman at the time.

Her physical ailments failed to capture the full impact of her struggle. Facing a 12-year sentence in an incapacitated state with no end in sight, she must have been on the brink of despair. In essence, her disorder governed every aspect of her life.

This woman experienced a daily struggle of ongoing rejection. In the Jewish culture at the time, she was considered ritually unclean. This limited her physical contact with others and provided her with little or no social life. If she touched anyone in the Jewish community, that person would be "unclean" for the rest of the day and would have to take a bath to wash off the contamination.

Imagine being ostracized by society and living with an affliction that caused you to be treated like a disease. Recently, my husband sent me this text after deplaning a flight to Dallas: "Guy next to me was afraid of germs. Swabbing everything with alcohol pads. Wore one rubber glove (like Michael Jackson)." My husband's experience sitting near a person with germophobia was likely similar to how the religious community treated this woman.

Her infirmity's impact on her marital status escalated her situation even more. Since it was a violation for men to sleep with women who had this condition, likely she was either single or divorced. Adding to the difficulty, Jewish men often divorced women who were incapable of bearing children.

Not only was she out of ideas, she may have also been out of money. Scripture reveals she "had suffered many things from many physicians" (Mark 5:26).

She had spent all of her hard-earned life savings on popular treatments of the day, but she only grew worse. Magic and sorcery were commonly attempted treatments for diseases in that time. Physicians in her first-century context also used a variety of ineffective herbal cures on their patients. Surgery was always the last resort because it was performed without anesthetic, often killing the patient instead of curing them.

Hope seems far away when your body becomes an enemy. As a person who struggled with insomnia for seven years, I can identify with the discouragement produced by chronic issues that seem never to improve.

Today, desperate people will still resort to almost any form of remedy to improve their appearance, ease health concerns, or limit the risk of diseases. In popular culture, for example, health and nutrition have become one of these remedies. The appeal of nutrition as a cure-all is undeniable in a society devoted to the trim, the fit, and especially the healthy. I recently saw a Facebook post boasting the health benefits of cucumbers. The title of the post was, "I Started Consuming Cucumber 3 Times Per Day As The Doctor Said, After 5 Days Something Changed."[1] Though there was no mention of exactly how cucumbers changed this person's life, the article offers a bulleted list of the vegetable's near-miraculous effects ranging from relieving joint pain to fighting cancer.

As an avid cucumber fan (especially the Persian ones from Trader Joe's), I remain convinced that fruits and vegetables are a necessary part of a healthy diet—even though I consume far too many Oreos and too much ice cream in a given week. However, cucumbers did not offer me the peaceful night's rest I desperately longed for when I struggled with insomnia. While up in the night, I would search Google and discover remedies like bananas, almonds, and cherry juice. However, this fruit salad of medications would have no results. Although I did experience an occasional bout of shut-eye from time to time, those periods of precious sleep were too few and far between.

Like the woman in the story who sought a cure for her condition, I attempted almost every proposed solution to overcome my zombie sleepless state. Over-the-counter sleeping pills allowed me to fall asleep temporarily, but did not offer me a deep sleep or the feeling of a night's rest the next day. My doctor gave me a long article explaining the nature of my insomnia and several lifestyle changes that were supposed to help. You name it, I tried it. I limited caffeine and sugar from my diet, and reduced time spent in front of computer and phone screens. I exercised. I committed to a schedule of going to bed at the same time every night. These are only a small selection of proposed solutions I considered.

Needless to say, I prayed for a breakthrough and sought God's perspective on my situation. I lived in constant state of what felt like jetlag: somewhere in between fully awake but not quite asleep. I grew concerned over how sleep deprivation was affecting my health.

It was as though my own bed had betrayed me. What should have served as an ideal, comfortable piece of furniture to give me a night's rest became a major source of stress to me. Like the suffering woman in the story, I exhausted all of my options and ran out of ideas.

I am constantly amazed over my husband's skill for repairing broken fixtures around the house. His secret? YouTube. These videos have given him instructions on almost every issue related to home repair. Have a problem? There's a YouTube video for it. However, a video does not actually have the power to fix anything, nor was YouTube available for our suffering friend in this biblical account. She couldn't repair her life on her own.

Often, we find ourselves in situations we cannot fix regardless of *how hard* we try or how many YouTube videos we watch. Sometimes the trials seem too overwhelming or complex and far outweigh our capacity to cope.

The first step to hope is a simple thought:

I can't fix this.

Amazingly, when all human resources failed her, the woman in the story refused to give in to her affliction. She did not allow her disease to form her identity. When she learned about Jesus' presence in her region, something outside of herself — a small seed of faith — began to emerge. She came to a life-changing decision: *If I can't fix this, I know someone who will.*

She was soon destined to discover the timeless truth about God: When our resources run out, it becomes an opportunity for Jesus to step in. He never runs out of anything — not even love.

The biblical author's account portrays this woman as a person of integrity. She did not ask Jesus for attention, money, power, wealth, or a position on His staff. Her only desire was to be well. She envisioned experiencing the same privileges every woman in her society took for granted — marriage, children, and above all *not* to be considered unclean.

For starters, the odds of successfully approaching Jesus were against her. With the large crowd clawing their way to Him, the chances of getting close were slim. Her self-consciousness over her disease could have undermined her confidence. She may have bought into the false notion that her condition would cause Jesus to be unclean.

She saw the mob gathering around Jesus, pressing into

him, each wanting His individual attention. But she was not about to give up—at least not yet. I can almost hear the wheels turning in this woman's mind. Upon noticing Jesus, she did not actually *ask* Jesus to heal her, but instead acted on her own initiative by moving toward him. Instead of pushing her way to Jesus like the rest of the crowd, she began to exercise her problem-solving skills.

This remarkable woman's ingenuity teaches one of the characteristics of hope that doesn't get much attention: *Hope thinks.* Hope has a mental capacity for working through obstacles by imagining the impossible.

Imagine the excited crowd, like cattle stampeding on an open range, as they trample their way past her to Jesus. Then, like the sun peeking through the thick layer of clouds after a storm, a ray of hope beams from inside of her. Out of the blue, she comes up with an idea: *I don't need to wrestle my way through this unruly mob to get close to Him.* "If only I may touch His garment, I shall be made well" (Matthew 9:21).

Knowing her next move, she gains the confidence to navigate through the crowd at a safe distance from Jesus, while just close enough to touch the edge of His robe. What seems like a small undertaking for a normal woman is a huge step for her. Her actions are bold in an environment of religious people who could single her out and expose her uncleanliness to the large crowd. Imagine the collective horror if they discover she had touched Jesus.

In the midst of her suffering, this out-of-options woman takes a chance on God's best idea. At the risk of being singled out by the crowd, she reaches out and grasps the robe of the One who can heal her. She can feel the texture of the fabric between her fingers as she clutches it firmly, for fear that the material may slowly slip through her hands. She grasps hold of God's best and greatest idea: Jesus.

Suddenly, this remarkable woman senses a dramatic change in her body. The moment she makes contact with Jesus' clothing, her bleeding ceases and she is instantly healed.

Jesus' reaction to her hands on His clothing startles her. She likely does not want to draw attention to herself. However, Jesus knows instantly that power has gone out from Him, which prompts a response the woman perhaps is unprepared for: "Who touched Me?" (Mark 5:31).

It is puzzling at first that Jesus singled her out. Can we assume He was unaware of who she was? Jesus is omnipotent, the One who knows all, and He was well aware of the identity of this woman trembling in His presence. Perhaps His purpose in drawing attention to her was to praise her publically for her faith.

We can reasonably assume that the woman thought she could find healing from Jesus' clothing itself, as if there was some kind of magic power in His garment. Common superstition at the time held that the power of a person could be transmitted through their apparel. However, Jesus does not say, "My clothing made you well!" or "Power has gone out from my robe!" Instead, He senses that power has gone out from His *person* and announces, "Daughter, your faith has made you well" (Mark 5:34). Through faith, even those who approach with their own ideas can encounter God's best idea.

Jesus is God's best idea. The greatest thought that ever entered God's mind was giving up His only Son Jesus. Who would bring Adam and Eve back into the garden again to walk with God in the cool of the day? How would humankind be redeemed from the sin that permanently corrupted human minds and hearts?

God's ideas were born out of His great love for us. God's idea to send His only Son in human flesh to walk among us was foremost in His mind from the beginning of time. Who but God could fathom a redemptive solution like Jesus' death and resurrection as an atonement for sin? Who but God could conceive a painfully grievous reality like sending His Son as a sacrifice on the cross for our sins in order to transform us into His image?

Jesus saw something greater in this helpless woman than a list of symptoms. She was more than a person who needed treatment; He saw something so remarkable in her that she caught His attention, causing Him to turn around and speak. In His eyes, she was not a victim of suffering. She was a woman of faith!

She was His daughter. His endearing words to his suffering child expressed affirmation of His love for her: "Daughter, your faith has made you well. Go in peace, and be healed of your affliction" (Mark 5:34). The word daughter was used as a term of acceptance and affection at the time. He thought of her as his daughter, in the same manner that He loves each woman as His daughter and welcomes her into His family.

God's best idea, Jesus, is keenly aware of the specific details of our circumstances. How Jesus, in spite of dwelling with us as a *man* when he walked the earth as God, is cognizant of the nature of suffering unique to *women* is worth noting. Through this woman's experience, Jesus' deep concern about every aspect of a woman's private pain and discomfort is obvious.

God's best idea is alive and well. I confess that after so many years of laying awake nights, I thought I was doomed to a state of sleeplessness for the rest of my life. To my surprise, God had another idea, beginning the night we arrived to our new location in Washington after a long drive from our former home in California. We arrived late in the afternoon to our temporary two-bedroom, unfurnished apartment near the university campus where my husband was beginning employment.

The moment I walked through the door of our new, empty apartment, I wondered how I was going to survive living with no furniture, much less no sleep. Our bed the first night was two sleeping bags on the hard, beige carpeted floor. As evening came and Earl and I settled down inside our sleeping bags, all was quiet. The silence was unlike the all too noisy neighborhood I had just move from, where it was common to hear police sirens and loud conversations on the street.

Then, the unthinkable happened. I closed my eyes, and suddenly I was out like a light. What just happened? It was the first real night of rest I had experienced in years. I slept like a baby all of that week and into the next. The pattern has continued. It was official. Although I have an occasional restless night, I recently announced to my friends that I am now a "sleeping person."

Perhaps the abrupt change in my sleeping habits was a result of my new environment. No longer facing the pressures of our former church hanging over my head, I flourished in my peaceful surroundings of tall pines, mountains, and Lake Washington just a few miles away. Jesus can use a variety of methods, even a change in environment, to make us whole. Rather than using a detailed formula in his encounters with people, He treats each person He heals in a unique manner.

Many of us have yet to see the miracle we need in our situation. At the time of writing this, I am struggling with another annoying physical issue. I need a miracle. With Jesus, there is no one size fits all. Jesus displays His power by a variety of means to make us whole. The suffering woman found this to be true when she refused to put Jesus in a box, but instead put her problem-solving skills to work in a creative way to reach Jesus.

The transforming story of the woman with the issue of blood is told in three out of four Gospels for a reason. She represents so many people who have exhausted their options and are out of ideas, like I was in the airport without my license and with my insomnia. She remains an example for all those whose tired hearts need the power of faith in Christ. Her stubborn hope in the power of Jesus (and even in His clothing) when all odds are against her, gives me hope.

I'm sure by now you are wondering if I ever made it to Milwaukee. Our first move at the airport was to limit the drama by approaching a security agent privately, avoiding humiliation in front of a whole line of passengers. Working through my dilemma with the airport security staff was a long process and involved searching for other forms of ID, an awkward private search with a female security staff, several phone calls by agents, and a thorough search inside my luggage. I was impressed with the detailed competence and overall efficiency of the airline security. In part, I felt grateful for their refusal to allow me an easy pass through security, even though I had a boarding pass in my hand.

After a mobile phone interrogation with a TSA person in Washington, DC politely quizzing me about facts like former addresses and neighbors (a few I didn't even remember), and making full use of a few of our negotiation skills, by God's grace and mercy I was allowed to board the plane! I made it to Madison. Of course, my return trip was much more complicated, but let's just say I made it back to Oakland.

Expect

To be the head and not the tail
The victor and not the victim
To forgive and be forgiven
To hope where there's despair
To experience comfort in tribulation
To find wisdom in the midst of confusion

To give and not lack

To be strong when I feel weak

To overcome and not be defeated

To be bold and not fearful

To dwell in peace amidst the storm

-Janet Creps

A Prayer

Dear Lord, I confess that I am out of ideas.

I am at a loss for where to go from here.

I have grown weary from thinking and stressing over my situation.

Thank you, Lord, that you are here with me.

Give me the faith I need to trust your healing power in my life.

Knowing you is the best idea I've ever thought of, even though the idea was yours from the beginning.

Thank you for the transformation that will take place in the near future and for your power at work in my life.

Thank you for your grace and love for me.

Questions for Reflection

- Describe the most significant challenge you face where you need a breakthrough.
- Read 2 Corinthians 4:8-18 and Luke 11:9-12. What is God showing you about His idea to help you in your dilemma?
- In what way does God encourage you when you feel little hope for your situation?

7

LYDIA

Hope Gives

"And when she and her household were baptized, she
begged *us*, saying,
'If you have judged me to be faithful to the Lord,
come to my house and stay'" (Acts 16:15 NKJV).

The first rule of thumb when boarding a subway train in
Tokyo is this: Get in the car. Now! Do not attempt to be
polite and let others rush in ahead of you. As a tourist from
the friendly Midwest, I learned this lesson the hard way. The
last time I visited this mammoth metropolitan railway, I was
almost stranded alone on the platform.

The incident happened when my husband and I, along
with our travelling companions, were about to step into a
subway car. Everything seemed fine until hoards of hurried

travelers pushed their way in front of me, instantly separating me from my companions. The crowd blocked my path through the train door. I could see the door begin to close in front of me as a flood of anxious commuters hurriedly shoved their way into the car. I felt doomed to be stranded alone in the abyss of Tokyo's subway system. I was saved at the last minute, however, as several Japanese passengers reached out their hands to pull me inside the car before the train slipped away into the dark tunnel. That was close!

Life requires a team effort. Sometimes we need to rely on the mercy of others to reach out and pull us into the subway car.

In the book of Acts, Luke writes about an influential woman named Lydia who stands out as one of those exceptional individuals who helps others board the train.

When you venture out to try something completely new, like riding a Tokyo subway train, you need a lot of Lydias in your life. The Apostle Paul learned this the hard way when he arrived in the port city of Troas on the eastern coast of the Aegean Sea. Paul's decision to journey to Macedonia was a process of ruling out where *not* to go, beginning with the Holy Spirit preventing him from preaching several times in the Roman province of Asia (Turkey). With all of the doors closed, he and his traveling ministry team found themselves in Troas all dressed up with no place to go. One night, Paul had a vision of a man from Macedonia who appeared to him saying, "Come over to Macedonia and help us" (Acts 16:9). The next day, he and his team began the sea voyage to Europe. A few days later, they arrived at the city of Philippi.

Although not mentioned in his letters, Paul's journey to Philippi may have begun with disappointment. Scholars tell us that the Roman empire at this time permitted its citizens to practice their own religions, but *not* to proselytize — making preaching in Philippi illegal.[1] The Macedonian man from Paul's dream was nowhere to be found!

Paul's sea adventure brought the good news about Jesus to Europe for the first time — a new thing! To accomplish this, Paul's band definitely needed a *lot* of help! Most likely, Paul began his mission in Philippi the same way he had in so many other cities — by looking for a synagogue. However, in Philippi, there wasn't one!

Instead, Paul found a group of women gathered to worship the God of Israel beside a river, probably in the open air. Evidently, the Jewish community in Philippi was so small at the time that it did not have the requisite quorum (a *minyan*) of ten men required to form a synagogue.

Within this group praying by the riverside, Paul was about to meet a special woman named Lydia who was destined to help him and bring hope for the new work God was about to do. Luke, one of Paul's traveling companions, describes this scene in Acts 16:

> And on the Sabbath day we went out of the city to the riverside, where prayer was customarily made; and we sat down and spoke to the women who met *there*. Now a certain woman named Lydia heard *us*. She was a seller of purple from the city of Thyatira, who worshiped God. The Lord opened her heart to heed the things spoken by Paul. And when she and her household were baptized, she begged *us*, saying, "If you have judged me to be faithful to the Lord, come to my house and stay." So she persuaded us (Acts 16:13-15).

What was so special about Lydia? She was from Thyatira in the Roman province of Asia, the part of the world Paul had just left to sail for Europe. She was a wealthy businesswoman, a seller of purple. The production of this unique dye was a costly process involving extensive labor and thousands of snails. Purple goods were the product of a luxury industry and were used by emperors, high government officials, and priests of pagan religions. Purple garments were the Gucci of their day. If the Academy Awards had been held in the first century, famous actresses and celebrities would have paraded the red carpet wearing costly purple gowns.

The greater community knew Lydia for more than her success in business. Her soft heart had a growing hunger for a deeper relationship with God. Luke refers to her as a worshipper of God, or "Godfearer": a term used to describe Gentiles who were not yet converts to Judaism, but who did worship the God of the Jews. Though identified as spiritual people, "Godfearers" were not yet part of the body of Christ which was made up of both Jewish and Gentile believers in Jesus the Messiah.

Lydia's life transformed when God opened her heart, bringing her into relationship with Him, and making her the first person recorded in Scripture to follow Christ in Europe. Lydia's conversion was only the beginning. Through her generous hospitality to offer Paul and his companions her home as the first gathering of believers, she made it possible to launch the church in Europe.

Interior decorating has become big business in the area where I live. Clusters of furniture stores are equipped with personal interior designers ready to make each house into a showcase. Lydia's gift of hospitality, however, offered something greater than name brand furniture. Rather than just a place for displaying fancy furnishings (which she may have owned), Lydia purposed for her home to be a place of hope. Her house would become a strategic location where empty hearts would be filled through relationship with Christ.

Like Lydia, God has created all of us to bring hope into our environments. Lydia's example shows us that hope is not limited to a state of well-being, but is a **gift**, a precious treasure destined to be given away. Anyone can become an encouragement to someone else. Those who struggle to find hope for themselves can always be the first to give it away.

God often commissions individuals like Lydia who have set their hearts on offering support to others. They are not necessarily people of means, wealth, or status, but they are people who God calls to partner with us in life's journey. God sends these key individuals to "flip the script," not only in your ministry and career, but in your personal life. I can only be as effective as the people who help me into the subway car and who keep me from being left at the station.

I can recall countless occasions and situations when God sent individuals like Lydia to sow encouragement in the key areas where I needed it the most. I dedicate this chapter to the game-changing Lydias who came onto the scene during challenging times of my life. They represent people whose generosity and inspiration made a huge difference in my life, ministry, and perhaps even destiny.

One of the first Lydias who comes to mind is my friend

Helen who opened the heart of her home to me in the 70s. At the time, I was a single young adult and longed to find a suitable young man who would one day become my spouse. Of course, I was filled with anxiety about whether I would find "the one" — that special significant other God created to become my partner in life.

One day I was lamenting my situation to Helen, who was married and several years older. I confessed my doubts to her about the future of my marital status. After several disappointing experiences with dating, I had come to the conclusion that I would never find a young man suitable to fill this empty place in my future. Making matters worse, I had become convinced that God would not fulfill the desire of my heart because I didn't have enough faith in Him.

Helen listened empathetically as I poured out my heart to her. Unlike some insensitive Christians I have known, she did not lecture me on the effect of doubt on one's spiritual growth. Instead, she offered the most life-giving words I have ever heard. Her wise, nurturing response went something like this: "Janet, don't worry about having faith for a husband because I have enough faith for both of us. Just rely on my faith."

Essentially, Helen reassured me that her faith and prayers would take over where mine left off. I didn't need to have enough faith for a future spouse because I was not alone. She would have faith for me.

About a year after our conversation, God brought a uniquely gifted young man into my world, who became my best friend and soon my husband-to-be. Who would have guessed that Helen would be a special guest at our wedding in my Wisconsin hometown? That was now over 40 years ago!

Helen's friendship illustrates how Christ destines us not only to seek hope for ourselves, but also to become the agents of hope for others. Without Lydias, our new church in Berkeley, for instance, would not have succeeded or even started. Berkeley was our Philippi. We embarked on something new in an unfamiliar place.

The first challenge in our start-up adventure was finding a place to live in California. We needed a miraculous sign to undertake this mission: a home in the same city where we were starting a church. The expense of renting in our area would not be an option for us and would consume most of the equity from the sale of our home in Missouri within a year.

We knew buying a home in the pricey Bay area would be a challenge, but I never anticipated the number of obstacles we would face. I almost gave up on our search after my first experience at an open house. It was my dream home—a cozy bungalow nestled in a grove of old trees, secluded in a quiet neighborhood. The beautiful and quaint home was an old Craftsman, painted white with a garden window in the kitchen. It reminded me of a dollhouse with built-in glass cabinets and a quaint (but non-functional) wood burning fireplace. The moment I walked in the door, I was in love. In my imagination, I moved right in and began to arrange my furniture. Once I realized the price, however, my heart sank. This was way more house than we had a budget for! My dream house quickly became a nightmare.

I darted out of the house to my car before anyone could see me cry. I was convinced our chances of owning a home in the Bay area were about like the odds of being recruited to play quarterback for the Pittsburgh Steelers.

Fortunately, I was wrong. When you run out of hope, hope will not run out on you. In the wake of our home buying despair, God brought us Mike, a real estate broker in the East Bay, through a friend's recommendation. When I finally found the courage to call him, his pleasant personality increased my confidence to explain our dire situation. We wanted to purchase a home in Berkeley, but had a limited amount of equity from the sale of our house to use for a down payment. Making matters worse, we had yet to be pre-qualified for a loan.

After a long, awkward pause, his first words were: "That area is pretty pricey." I thought to myself, *Well, at least I tried.*

I would not have blamed him if he turned me down flat. It was unreasonable to assume he would take us on as clients with so few qualifications. Surprisingly, though, Mike agreed to work with us! He became our Lydia in that season. Needless to say, our pursuit of a home was met with dozens of set-backs, and for a while we thought it would never happen. The financial crisis of 2008 made house shopping a difficult experience for many people.

In spite of being turned away by several banks, experiencing numerous dead-end house searches, and having contracts fall through, we finally bought our bank-owned home on the very same street as the house I had cried over months before. Somehow, through the miracle of a church offering, we were able to pay the closing costs.

Upon moving in, we discovered that we were not the only ones who needed hope. Our "new" house was in rough condition. Built in 1926, when Calvin Coolidge was president, our home looked like the before house on a fixer-upper reality show. It was an eyesore, painted a dirty Pepto-Bismol pink with dated aluminum windows throughout.

All of the appliances were old, dirty, or non-functional. We cooked our meals on a George Foreman grill for the first several months. The electrical outlets were antiques and the furnace was on its last leg. That was just the inside of the house. The backyard was overrun with a carpet of smelly wild onions. Every time we cut the grass, the entire yard smelled like French onion soup.

The odds that we would be able to make our house actually livable seemed dismal at best. Fortunately, not everyone shared our opinion. One Sunday, we shared our vision for our city at an adult Sunday school class in Santa Ana, California. We were unaware that five experienced carpenters were in the audience listening attentively and were about to turn our home upside down. While we shared our story with the class, God was working on their hearts to come to Berkeley and renovate our house. They would become our Lydias with tools.

It wasn't long before these men were on their way to Oakland in a private plane to assess the damage. When they inspected our house, they were appalled at its condition. They were especially concerned that our front door only had duct tape over the hole where the lock should have been.

Several days later, our carpenter friends returned with a truckload of tools to work on the repairs. They replaced windows and doors, fixed electrical problems and the heater, and even put in a ceiling light over our dining room table. Their help made our very run-down house livable.

As with any start-up adventure, finding a place to live is only the beginning. We needed to find a name for our church, so we decided to call it 360church. Our pastor friends from Ireland suggested the name. We were unsure how the number 360 applied to our church and mission, but it was the only name we could think of. We decided to keep it until we found a better one.

Of course, selecting a name is not the most difficult challenge when starting a church. We needed people! Contrary to our initial strategy of bringing an excited team of Christians to come with us, we arrived in Berkeley alone. Earl and I were the only attendees of 360church. We were disappointed to discover that most of the individuals we had recruited to partner with us backed out at the last minute.

The first few months in our new surroundings were very memorable. Having just arrived and not knowing anyone, we contemplated what to do for Easter Sunday. Should we celebrate the holiday by attending a church in our area, or should we bite the bullet and do a pre-launch Easter service in faith? We decided on the latter. On Easter morning, Earl and I found a spot at the entrance of the UC Berkeley campus and started our "service." The campus was mostly deserted, with the exception of our first visitor: a tiny brown finch flitting about at our feet. Our Easter service was likely the shortest church service ever. We sang a hymn, Earl read a text from Scripture, and then we prayed.

However, we were soon to meet our next group of

Lydias in the days ahead. In the same way that Lydia became a key player in Europe by helping Paul and his colleagues, the men and women we encountered during the next few months became the heart of our lives and ministry.

Our ministry began with a police invasion of our home. I was watching television and talking on the phone one late afternoon when three armed police officers knocked at our front door. They warned me of reports (which turned out to be false) that armed teenagers may have invaded our backyard, and asked if they could search our property. The instant I invited them in, they stormed through the living room and kitchen and headed toward the back door.

In the middle of this drama, I was chatting on the phone with a student from UC Berkeley named Malia. Malia was a freshman I had never met who just happened to call right before the police arrived. She was unaware of the uproar going on in my home. I didn't mention any of it for fear of scaring her away. She had heard about what we were doing and was interested in knowing more about our new church.

The next step in the relationship was to invite Malia and her brother, who was also a student at UC Berkeley, for a casual dinner at our home. As we discussed our vision with them, they agreed to be the first visitors at a new weekly Bible study in our home. It wasn't long before Malia brought her student friends with her, adding a few more faces to our small group.

We started our church using a strategy everyone loves: eating. I made "comfort food" for those attending our Bible study. The menu was mainly chicken and dumplings, pasta from Costco, or Little Caesars pizza.

After adding a few more students from the campus and other young adults who somehow found us, we ran out of room in our dining room and moved our Bible study into the living room. This group included a few key individuals instrumental in launching the beginning stages of our new church. Like Lydia, they brought what we needed the most: the gift of hope.

If we were to grow into a healthy church, however, we needed more than people. We needed a committed team to take on responsibility. Many of the people in our original core group were occupied with other commitments. Although we were grateful for their support, this left us high and dry without the leadership we needed to move forward.

God often works behind the scenes on people's hearts when we least expect it, calling individuals like Lydia to participate in what He is doing. We soon realized that help was on the way as we discovered the people attending gatherings in our home were ready to go to work. Natasha was a talented graduate student from UC Berkeley who came to us on the recommendation of a pastor friend.

Originally from Uruguay, she was intelligent, bilingual, diligent, and a gifted leader. Although joining us would involve a 25-mile commute each week for her, she took the plunge anyway and became part of our team.

After months of meeting in our home, we moved our gathering to Sunday mornings at a rented hotel conference room with large windows facing a sidewalk. It is impossible to describe Natasha's role in our new church because she did everything! It is unfortunate that Natashas cannot be cloned and distributed to churches all over America. One of Natasha's amazing qualities was her continued loyalty to what we were doing, regardless of our church's endless challenges. She became the worship leader, keyboard player, treasurer, and filled in the countless gaps in our embryonic organization.

A young man named Jeff became another important part of our life and 360church. Every church needs to have a fun "cool guy." Jeff was that guy. He brought a large personality to the group, and everyone liked him. Jeff's charisma was crucial since Earl and I were decades older than our congregation. Never having visited the San Francisco area before, he was willing to drop everything and move to Berkeley to be a part of our team. He came at his own risk and found a place to live. Jeff became our associate pastor, emcee, and event coordinator among other roles. After Jeff married, his wife Ericka became another wonderful friend and great asset to the ministry.

As we began 360church, a gifted young couple named Marc and Semra also moved to the area to start a ministry specifically for Cal students. They became the answer to our prayers, willingly serving in key leadership roles both on campus and in our church. As a result of Marc and Semra's ministry on the campus, other students became a part of our team—individuals like Randy, who was dedicated to God and willing to serve. From making coffee on Sunday mornings to carrying sound equipment up several flights of stairs, there was nothing that Randy could not or would not do.

We never knew what to expect on a given Sunday. Like any entrepreneurial experience, church planting can prove unpredictable, especially in weekly attendance. One Sunday, Earl, Jeff, and our campus pastors were all out of town. The remaining handful of our regular attendees were absent due to other commitments, leaving only me and Natasha. I was reluctant to cancel the service for fear that someone would show up unexpectedly.

Since we were not sure who would attend, we prepared for two scenarios: plan A and plan B. Plan A was designed for three or more persons attending. We would set up tables, chairs, and coffee for our usual service, open with prayer, and continue with singing an acapella song from the lyrics on a handout. Singing would be followed by a teaching, which I would share from a section of Scripture also printed on handouts. We would close the service by offering to pray for individual concerns. We would enact plan B if only two of us showed up. Natasha and I would have coffee and spend the service time praying together.

Not surprisingly, the room was empty at 11:00 a.m. Natasha and I chatted over coffee for several minutes on the chance that walk-ins might arrive. After 15 minutes, the decision had been made for us. We would launch plan B, have more coffee, pray together, and maybe go out for lunch.

Natasha and I had been praying for about 20 minutes when a young student from UC Berkeley arrived. After a warm greeting, I invited him to join us and concluded that we would now transition to plan A for the "real" service, including the Scripture lesson I had planned. Later, we would call this particular day "Awkward Sunday," and it became infamous. There would be many more "Awkward Sundays" ahead, but this one was especially memorable.

Following Natasha, Mark, and Semra, there were several other quality individuals who served as Lydias and shared our vision for the city of Berkeley. Most were students from the University of California who partnered with us on our journey by assisting us with worship, sound equipment, hospitality, emceeing, or anything else we needed. They became our assistant pastors, worship leaders, and teachers. These key influencers not only gave us hope, but also became an inspiration to us and the city. I am unsure how we would have accomplished anything without them. A few, like Alan and Amy, stayed with us until we moved to Washington.

Overall, the story of Lydia's generosity offers a personal challenge: Is God calling me to bring hope to someone else? Often the answer to prayer is a person, and that person could be me. Perhaps my search for hope will lead me to cultivate specific ways to I can bring tangible hope to others. Small actions like sharing an encouraging word, practicing hospitality, and giving out of a generous heart can make a big difference in the lives of others.

The greatest opportunity to become Lydias happens at home as we sow affirmation in the lives of those closest to us—our family, spouse, or children. My husband has taken on the role as the most significant Lydia in my world. His deep love and devotion, tender affection, and constant affirmation have been a constant source of strength and encouragement.

Scripture teaches, "Let each of you look out not only for his own interests, but also for the interests of others"

(Philippians 2:4).

Natural inclination assumes if I invest in the interests of others, I will fall short of accomplishing my own personal goals. In fact, the opposite stands true. We watched God open doors for many of our supporters who helped serve our church. This is not to say life awards immediate success to those who willingly serve God and others. Paul and his fellow workers experienced numerous trials and sufferings in their journey. Yet, as He was with Paul, God remains faithful to honor those who serve him.

Hope will often thrive in a cycle. When your heart is too weak to exercise hope, God can bring it to you and then you can offer it to someone else, who can do the same. At the beginning of 2 Corinthians, Paul describes this cycle from his own experience:

Blessed *be* the God and Father of our Lord Jesus Christ, the Father of mercies and God of all comfort, who comforts us in all our tribulation, that we may be able to comfort those who are in any trouble, with the comfort with which we ourselves are comforted by God (2 Corinthians 1:3-4).

Ultimately, the true source of hope is Christ, who calls ordinary people to reveal His love and concern. Somewhere, someone is praying for help. Every time we sow hope into someone's life, we enter into a powerful transforming cycle that also positions us to be its recipients. **Hope gives.**

A Prayer

Lord, thank you for reaching out to me

with your unfathomable love and endless generosity

when my faith was weary and I needed hope.

Thank you Jesus for offering me

your abundant grace in every moment of my life.

Thank you for welcoming me into your presence

the same way Lydia welcomed Paul and his companions

into her home.

Open my heart to receive your words to me,

as you did for Lydia when she heard Paul's news about your love.

Help me to become an ambassador of hope to those who are in despair.

Lead me to those who are praying for encouragement and help

in the midst of their circumstances.

Thank you that your door is always open at every moment,

and you are only a prayer away.

Questions for Reflection

- Name those individuals who have functioned as Lydias in your life. What difference did they make?
- Read 2 Corinthians 9:6-8. What does God promise to do for those who give with a cheerful heart?
- Are you the answer to someone's prayer? If so, whose? What specific ways can you encourage them?

8

MARY MAGDELENE

Hope Weeps

"Woman, why are you weeping?" (John 20:13 NKJV)

The incident began late one morning. I was typing on my laptop at our kitchen table while looking out the glass door at the forest in our backyard.

We live in a wooded development east of Seattle where our back deck faces a cluster of tall pine and cedar trees. This forest is home to wild animals like deer, coyotes, and bobcats. I have even occasionally seen bears in our backyard. A few months ago, I caught one guzzling sugar water from our hummingbird feeder!

With so many predators around, we rarely leave our

wire terrier Ricky outside alone. That particular day, he was clipped securely to a long leash tied to our deck, which was about thirty feet away and in plain view of my seat in the kitchen.

Suddenly, I heard his bark and instantly looked out of the window to discover the source of the commotion. Before I knew what was happening, Ricky had broken out of his harness and headed into the woods to chase a wild animal. Seconds later, I heard his distant cries telling me of a bloodcurdling altercation with the intruder. Then silence. He was gone.

In desperation, I called out my little dog's name several times, hoping the sound of my voice would lead him out of the woods and back where he belonged. I could only hear the buzzing traffic on the windy road below the plateau of our backyard.

I frantically wrestled my way through dense vegetation and clung to spindly groves of young pine trees, hoping to catch any sign of him. The sharp thorns from the wild blackberry bushes tore at my clothing. I struggled to keep my feet from sliding on the slippery clay coated with wet leaves and pine needles—but he was gone.

Our little dog was no more. All of our attempts to contact animal shelters, hospitals, and neighbors gave us no information. Ironically, the incident occurred while I was in the middle of writing this chapter at my kitchen table.

My husband and I came to the horrifying conclusion that the wild animal that carried Ricky off was most likely a coyote. They are common where we live and some of our neighbors have seen them roaming the area. I learned that coyotes in our area are more aggressive than in other regions and have been known to attack small animals — apparently including terriers.

Ricky fell far short of being a "Best in Show," well-groomed, fancy designer dog that proud owners parade at exclusive resorts and upscale shopping centers. In spite of all of our efforts to bathe him and keep him clean, he looked a lot like the dirty lamb's wool hand duster in our laundry room closet with his long, stiff white fur.

Our terrier's big personality eclipsed his little 11-pound body. He was fun, smart, lovable, and completely annoying. Even though his incessant barking and constant demands on our time were irritating, he wormed his way into our hearts with his endearing affection, cute tricks, and silly chase games created to lure us into playing with him.

More importantly, I have never known a happier pet than Ricky. He could hardly contain his joy and excitement over the simplest and most uneventful dog experiences. He was overjoyed at the thought of going for a walk, riding in the car, or consuming particles of any kind of food that would occasionally fall on the kitchen floor. Ricky was the only dog I ever encountered who delighted in pouncing on warm laundry right out of the dryer.

Now that our dog is gone, I cannot bring myself to cry for some reason. His black metal crate and water bowl are still in their place on the tile floor of our laundry room. We are still vacuuming up pieces of white fur, little reminders of his presence.

I know I am not alone in my need to find a way to process grief. The hurt feels like combing the woods, hoping to find what was lost.

Hope grieves. I am convinced that what many hurting people need is a good cry. We all require the solace only found through this special healing liquid. There is a comforting power in tears that allows us to process our pain and hurt, and eventually helps us to feel better.

The significance of tears can be traced back thousands of years to biblical times. The amount of weeping documented in the Bible is amazing. Many Old Testament stories feature this kind of drama. In fact, an entire book in the Old Testament is entitled Lamentations.

Perhaps people who lived thousands of years ago understood the importance of crying. Public weeping was commonplace in Jewish culture. For example, David and his followers wept over his son Absalom's rebellion when he attempted to steal the kingdom away from his father, resulting in David's escape for his life from his home in Jerusalem. The Apostle Paul's companions wept together as he prepared to depart for Jerusalem, not knowing if they would ever see him again.

At other times, weeping was more of a private affair. Job was distraught over his multiple trials: "My face is flushed from weeping, And on my eyelids *is* the shadow of death" (Job 16:16). Joseph, upon seeing his younger brother Benjamin after so many years apart, hid himself in a private place to cry. As we all know, Jesus wept at the tomb of Lazarus.

Moreover, the prophets utilized images of weeping women to communicate national suffering. Jeremiah, for example, describes the figure of Rachel "weeping for her children, Refusing to be comforted for her children, Because they *are* no more" (Jeremiah 31:15). The Apostle Matthew quotes this passage as prophetic of King Herod's reign of terror in the killing of male infants in Bethlehem after Jesus' birth (Matthew 2:18).

At the forefront of these accounts in Scripture are powerful stories of women. Hannah cried out in her brokenness for God to give her a child. Mary Magdalene wept at Jesus' tomb, and her experience offers significant insight about tears and the role they play in our lives.

Mary Magdalene, the focus of this chapter, was not a stranger to grief. A devoted follower of Jesus, she watched Him tried, condemned, and worst of all, killed on a cross. As far as Mary Magdalene knew, her life as a follower of Jesus seemed to be over. Not long before His death, she was still serving Him along with a group of many women who supported Jesus out of their own means. Now, He was out of her life completely. She arrived at Jesus' tomb only to find an empty grave. Where could He be? An unnamed poet describes her devotion:

> Not she with traitorous kiss her Master stung,
> Not she denied Him with unfaithful tongue;
> She, when Apostles fled, could dangers brave,
> Last at the Cross, and earliest at the grave.[1]

As Mary mourned over her beloved friend, imagine her surprise when she discovered two angels clothed in white sitting near where Jesus' body had lain. Their surprising question "Why are you weeping?" must have seemed inappropriate and out of place considering that Mary had a good reason to cry. She was one of Jesus' devoted followers. This amazing Jesus, who was so precious to her and had transformed her life by setting her free from several demons, was supposed to be in His tomb.

Now, He was missing. It was bad enough that His body would not be anointed with the spices she had brought with her to His grave. She was robbed of the opportunity to say goodbye and find the closure she needed to move.

As a result, Mary was overcome with grief when she discovered that Jesus' body was gone. Her depth of sorrow could not be contained in a quiet display of emotion. In the ancient language of this passage, the word used for weep refers to expressions that are "uncontainable, audible grief, weeping aloud."[2] Like standing under the brute force of a towering waterfall, she was overtaken by the amazing phenomenon we call tears.

Mary's reaction to the mystery of Jesus' missing body depicts a common response to pain and suffering: tears. Infants are equipped with the instinct to cry the moment they are born. Most of us have experienced this form of waterworks at one time or another.

It seems rather odd that God would endow us with this peculiar experience of tiny currents of salty liquid flowing from our eyes. He could have simply left us to process our feelings using more practical methods like talking, thinking things through, or exercising. According to legend, tears were thought to heat the heart, which generated water vapor in order to cool itself down. The heart's vapor would then rise to the head, condense near the eyes, and escape as tears.

Although the purpose of tears remained a mystery throughout the ages, the modern "science of crying" now offers several theories for the purpose and benefit of tears. First, crying serves as a means of expressing feelings from the innermost places of our heart. Scientists believe tears "trigger social bonding and human connection."[3] One theorist, Jonathan Rottenberg, indicates: "Crying signals to yourself and other people that there's some important problem that is at least temporarily beyond your ability to cope."[4] Crying releases a comforting form of communication that occurs when all other options fail to express our pain.

Second, tears help us feel better. Emotional tears are chemically different from the ones people shed while chopping onions. They are a healthy and safe form of expressing the emotions bottled up inside of us. Through this consoling form of expression, we can process our pain and anxiety, and even our joys and celebrations. In Mary Magdalene's case, there was no language to express her deep heartbreak. Simply put, sometimes words are not enough, so God created tears.

According to William Frey, "crying is a stress reliever, and unrelieved stress can hasten heart disease and kill brain cells....Crying helps us survive."[5] Though opinions on the health effects of tears may be mixed, studies have investigated the influence of crying on relationships. One recent study found:

> ...noncrying people had a tendency to withdraw and described their relationships as less connected. They also had experienced more negative aggressive feelings, like rage, anger and disgust, than people who cried. Tears bring release from the tensions inside of us...Often a person is unaware of what is inside until you cry it out.[6]

One of the most significant struggles I faced in my pastoral ministry in our church start-up was my inability to cry—although not at first. During the first couple of years in our journey, crying came easy. Crying was a natural outlet for the stress we faced.

One Sunday morning on my way to the hotel where our church gathered, I was searching for a place to park in the pouring rain. Earl was out of town speaking at a church while I was driving our Volvo loaded with the bulky equipment needed for the service—signs, instruments, microphone stands, and speakers to name a few. When I finally found a spot about a quarter of a block away, the people I had counted on to help unload my vehicle had not yet arrived. The thought of being abandoned with a boatload of heavy equipment in a heavy rain was more than

I could handle, so I did what came naturally. I cried. Fortunately, after waiting in my car for several minutes, friends arrived to help and were unaware of my meltdown.

After a few years, however, the emotional stress of growing a few people into a healthy church began to accumulate and crying became more of a challenge. Eventually, my tears were nonexistent. The following is an account from my journal:

> One of the greatest tragedies … is that I can't even cry anymore. It scares me. Is my heart that hard? I think I am just numb. But I really need to cry. I need to find some tears in the well of my soul. I need to find some way to allow a few more drops to help make me feel better.

We faced one of our worst experiences not long after our church moved to a theater in downtown Berkeley. One Sunday morning, we arrived early to set up and were informed that Stan, the theater manager and a significant part of our community, had committed suicide. He had met with us every Sunday to help us with the production side of the service and had been an emotional support to what we were doing. I was completely devastated over losing Stan, but the tears I kept inside for him refused to come. I simply could not "just cry it out."

The purpose of crying goes beyond processing our emotions. Up close, tears are fascinating pieces of art. Artist and photographer Rose-Lynn Fischer discovered a unique way to explore tears through photography. The title of an article written about her asks, "The Tears of Rose Lynn Fisher: What Do Sadness and Joy, Laughter and Longing Look Like Up Close?" Fisher simply "began photographing her tears under a microscope because she had been crying a lot and wondered what they'd look like up close."[7] She started by putting her own tears on slides and observing what they looked like when magnified. Fisher describes her photographs:

"You're trying to bring words through into something that's wordless, trying to describe something that exists perfectly well on its own. The thing with crying is that so often the very power of the moment is precisely because you can't talk."[8]

Fisher's work shows us that tears might seem simple, but they are complex things carrying many meanings. The article describes her work:

"When Fischer saw the magnified tears for the first

time, there was a strange, almost overwhelming sense of awe. There were patterns, and there were shapes, and there were strange striations, Geometry, broken and unbroken, walls and fortresses. Bubbles, bursting apart, forming coastlines."[9]

The divine works of art Fischer discovered in her tears reveal the healing significance of this unique form of expression.

Beyond helping us to feel better and offering astonishing microscopic art, crying helps us to pray. Mary's encounter with the angels at Jesus' tomb serves as only one example of individuals who experienced encounters with God through their tears. You may be familiar with the story of Hannah, who longed for a child. In "bitterness of soul," Hannah "prayed to the Lord and wept in anguish" (1 Samuel 1:10). Not surprisingly, the Lord met her in the midst of her grief and granted her request.

Other examples in Scripture include Hezekiah, who wept bitterly after God informed him that his life was at an end. Upon observing Hezekiah's grief, God's heart was softened, and He promised him: "I have heard your prayer, I have seen your tears; surely I will heal you" (2 Kings 20:5). In many of his psalms, David weeps as he empties out his heart before God: "Hear my prayer, O Lord, And give ear to my cry; Do not be silent at my tears" (Psalm 39:12).

God sees our tears. The angels were well aware of Mary Magdalene's grief as she mourned over Jesus' missing body. Scripture records that in the midst of her lament, "she turned around and saw Jesus standing *there*, and did not know that it was Jesus" (John 20:14). When she finally recognized Jesus, Mary was so overcome with joy that she could not let him go.

Mary Magdalene's story of tears serves as a powerful reminder that Jesus is standing right beside us in the heartbreaks of our lives to bring us comfort and to let us know that He is alive!

Surprisingly, my relationship with Jesus as a young adult (as described in a previous chapter) actually began with weeping. One day, I was on the brink of tears while sitting on a dock next to my apartment in Newport Beach, thinking about the futility of my so-called life. Every void I tried to fill with relationships, success, and religion left me empty. To make things worse, I was flat broke and could not pay my rent. All my attempts to find a full-time job and generate an income to pay my living expenses had failed. My despair reached its peak when I had to give away my cat. I had run out of money to buy her food.

As I contemplated my state of hopelessness, I could feel the dam holding back my feelings of desperation for so long begin to crack. A flood of tears poured out of me, like the ocean breaking into a sinking ship. It wasn't long before my tears were in control, and there was no stopping them. The longer I wept, the more the tears came out of a vast, deep reservoir reserved for this destined event.

All at once, the tears I was shedding were not my own. I knew something enveloped me that was greater than myself. I felt as if someone or something was weeping through me. This experience became the turning point in my spiritual life, and after a few weeks, I turned my life over to Jesus and entered into a relationship with Him. Looking back, I realize that it was the Holy Spirit mourning through me, though at the time I didn't understand who the Holy Spirit was.

Finally, our tears give us hope. God never ignores our prayers. "You number my wanderings," writes the psalmist David. "Put my tears into Your bottle; Are *they* not in your book?" (Psalm 56:8). God takes note of every tear we cry. He welcomes us into His presence to be strengthened and healed. When we weep, we are praying.

Our dog Ricky never returned, and I miss him every day. I still hope he will show up at our front door, but I know that in some form Jesus is standing ready to meet me, not only in this loss, but in all the times when I needed Him the most.

The power of tears can draw us into God's presence.

Mary found Jesus' stubborn hope through her grief and sadness. Her experience at the empty tomb transformed her from a solemn grave visitor to a joyful witness of Jesus' resurrection. Mary's tears at the tomb speak for all people who are weeping and wondering where their Jesus is. Mary reminds us that Jesus is standing right beside us asking, "Why do you weep?" because He is right here with us.

Go ahead and weep. Cry your cares away. You will feel better. Moreover, Jesus will meet you there and may ask you the same question the angel asked Mary.

The best part of weeping is that it comes with a wonderful promise. The psalmist David encourages all who weep that "Weeping may endure for a night, But joy *comes* in the morning" (Psalm 30:5). If you are broken and sorrowful today, don't walk the forest looking for what is gone. Look forward to the joy that tomorrow will bring.

A Prayer

Thank you Jesus for comfort through your gift of tears.

You have counted them one by one and hold them in your bottle.

Release those tears inside that are yet to be born.

Let me find hope and solace in the unfailing love you have for me.

I give you my grief, sorrows, and losses,

and wait for your promise to turn my night of weeping
into your joy in the morning.

Questions for Reflection

- Is there a loss in your life where you need to grieve?
  If so, what is it?
- What support networks are available for you to work
  through your loss? Is there a friend who you can
  trust to talk to?
- Read John 20:11-18. How did Jesus bring new hope
  into Mary's life?
- Read Psalm 30, Isaiah 6:1-4, and Mathew 5:2-10.
  What does God promise to do for those who are
  heartbroken?

9

JESUS

Hope the Person

"Blessed *be* the God and Father of our Lord Jesus Christ,
who according to His abundant mercy has begotten us again
to a living hope through the resurrection of Jesus Christ
from the dead… " (I Peter 1:3 NKJV)

Everyone needs someone trustworthy. I could not really trust my terrier, who unfortunately passed away recently. He could not behave like one of the pampered designer breeds on TV, obediently trotting alongside their owners at the American Kennel Club championships. On the other hand, our scruffy, longhaired white dog Ricky was an endearing companion. He craved attention, loved children, and was crazy about the beach. He was the constant in our lives. At home. In the car. At the mall. Constant. And of course, I loved my dog—I just couldn't trust him.

We trained Ricky to the point where 95% of the time, he would obey our orders. It's that last 5% that really concerned me! He ran ahead of us once at the marina to visit a family eating lunch on the grass, and paused casually to poop on the grass next to their blanket and food! At the beach in San Francisco, he ran off after a seagull and disappeared. After a frantic search, we found him at a nearby marsh covered with mud. Another day, he followed a dog walker wrangling several happy pooches because he was carrying a large bag of dog treats in his pants pocket. There's that 5%.

Trust is more of an issue when it comes to people. For instance, can you name at least five people you trust? Okay, how about four? Three? If you can't find three, two, or even one person you can trust, perhaps you are not alone.

A lot of hope issues are really trust issues. If we cannot put our faith in our relationships with people, how can we have hope? I know from too many experiences how trusted relationships can lead to disappointment. Sadly, I learned to be cautious early in life. I grew up in a small town in Wisconsin where trust was never an issue. We only locked our doors at night. Parents allowed their children to play and roam all over the neighborhood unsupervised. Crime was basically nonexistent. No child wore a helmet on a bike or a seatbelt in a car. My sheltered Norman Rockwell-esque childhood resembled a television comedy out of the 1950s like *Leave it to Beaver,* with the exception of when June Cleaver would greet the Beaver with a glass of milk and plate of cookies when he came home from school. That never happened to me.

An unwritten code of ethics governed the relationships in my community. Authority figures like parents, teachers, police officers, and pastors were to be revered and respected without question. Friends were assumed to be loyal and true. However, after countless disappointing experiences with people I knew, my Disneyland worldview began to unravel. Not surprisingly, I developed trust issues later in life because of these situations. Needless to say, I am not alone in this experience.

Whom can we trust? These days, many Americans are wondering the same thing. Public trust in the government remains at a near historic low. According to Pew Research, only 19% of Americans today say they can trust the government in Washington to do what is right "just about always" (3%) or "most of the time" (16%).

One researcher writes about young adults' experiences with trust: "Millennials don't trust you. Why should they? They've grown up in a world in which traditional institutions and precepts have proved untrustworthy.

According to the Pew Research Center, just 19% of Millennials say most people can be trusted, compared with 31% of Gen Xers and 40% baby boomers."[1]

Lack of trust has become a dilemma for women especially. When it comes to relationships with the opposite sex, women across the country are wondering whom they can trust. Numerous reports of sexual assaults involving celebrities and movie mongrels have taken center stage in the media. Scandals involving men in the public eye are springing up like dandelions. I cannot imagine the terrible suffering and trauma that victims of these heinous crimes face.

One can reasonably conclude that an epidemic of distrust exists in our country. According to a journalist from *USA Today*, Americans do not trust one another anymore: "We're not talking about the loss of faith in big institutions such as the government, the church or Wall Street, which fluctuates with events. For four decades, a gut-level ingredient of democracy — trust in the other fellow — has been quietly draining away." Further research indicates that only one third of Americans say they trust others. That's a record low since 1972 when the survey first began.[2]

I am not entirely convinced that our country has sold out to this form of despair towards humanity. If this were true, airports would not be so crowded during the holidays. In spite of occasional disasters, the crowds of passengers continue to put their confidence in the pilots and airline crews to bring them to their destinations (with one exception: people like me who are afraid of flying, but fly anyway).

One need not be an expert to identify common sources of broken trust. I am convinced that the ability to bond in relationships begins developing at birth. A tiny infant will instinctively attach to his or her mother the moment she holds the child in her arms. For that innocent infant, trust is instinctive until it's broken.

For most people, whether to trust or not hinges on past experiences. Betrayals from family, spouses, friends, and employers to name a few have the potential to leave scars. It only takes one person to turn your safe world upside down. Like housebreaking a wild animal, restoring such a broken place in one's heart becomes a serious challenge.

My happiest memories as a child are the Sundays I spent at my grandmother's house in Minneapolis playing with the frisky, adorable, long-haired kittens that roamed her home. We looked forward to each time her long-haired, black and white house cat gave birth to a new litter of little creatures, and we would enjoy a delightful time with them until my grandmother found new homes for them.

We had so much fun with our little furry friends, until

something changed one day. Instead of giving birth in the house as usual, the mother cat instead had her litter in my grandparent's detached garage where the kittens remained confined. With little exposure to the outside world, the kittens became wild and fearful. Each time my siblings and I entered the garage they ran away and hid. This was especially frustrating for me. The kittens did not understand that my only intention was to pick them up, hold them close to me, and stroke their fluffy fur. However, these new kittens did not trust me.

My experience with the startled cats exemplifies how suspicion can creep into relationships. Perhaps you can identify with a frightened kitten that grew up in an old garage. The idea of taking risks on close relationships with others can be unsettling.

I am grateful for the special people in my life whose friendships and loyalty I can always count on, but people are imperfect and things pass away. Unmet expectations or distressing experiences take their toll on one's faith in humanity. Nevertheless, healthy relationships are necessary for an individual's continued wellbeing. Unless people feel confident to lean on others, trust issues can limit them in relationships and in life.

Somehow, we have to find a way out of the garage and back into the house.

Fortunately, trust that can be broken can also be rebuilt. We all have a starting point available to us where we can begin to heal and be restored. For those who have faced disappointments or trauma in relationships, quick solutions for long-term struggles sound insensitive and shallow. However, *somewhere* in our brokenness lies an ember of hope for healing.

Hope is a Person. For me, the person of the Lord Jesus has become my *somewhere*. The same hope and the same trust relationship that Jesus built with His followers when He walked on earth is available to us. This relationship can train us for all other relationships. The question remains: Why do people find trusting Jesus to be so implausible? Sadly, I have met several young adults who live with this question. When my husband and I became pastors of our downtown Berkeley church, a group of disenfranchised young people would camp out on Sundays on the sidewalk of the movie theater where we held our services, right in front of a Starbucks. From the way they were dressed and the good condition of their bicycles, it was clear they were not among the homeless population. They sat on the cold cement and made a living space out of lawn chairs, old blankets, and a large old boom box. Their large, mixed breed dogs would lie next to them. One girl, Mackenzie, sometimes brought her hula hoop with her and would twirl to the beat of loud rap music.

The first time I invited them to join us in a Sunday service, they snapped at me. One young man in particular, thin with uncombed long brown hair, became immediately hostile and expounded in great detail on how Christianity was a form of brainwashing. As far as he was concerned, he was finished with both God and all of the Christians who had disappointed him. He did not go into detail, which made it impossible for me to understand the source of his bitter experience. Clearly, he had lost whatever trust he may have once had with God.

My young street friends serve as examples of how disappointing faith in Christ can seem when viewed through the distorting lens of loveless "Christians." Understandably, my new friends were deprived of the opportunity to learn the real Jesus, at least for a season.

Placing your faith in someone you do not know is difficult. When I first met my husband Earl many years ago, I was instantly impressed with how stylish he looked. Today's fashion police now have a name for his ensemble: "matchy-matchy." He was sporting a navy blue polyester suit with red stitching, accompanied by a red striped shirt and a lipstick red tie—not to mention the coordinating navy blue leather platform shoes with red trim and laces. He was a 1970s fashion icon. For various reasons back then, I wasn't quite ready to take the marital plunge. I needed to know him personally and build a relationship of trust and friendship.

Similarly, I need to know Jesus personally if am to put my trust in him. For those who have been through negative experiences in relationships and are disenchanted with religion, the critical question at hand concerning Jesus is: *Why should I trust Him?*

The best way to evaluate someone is often to observe his or her behavior. Starbucks has a unique way of interviewing for barista positions. They avoid asking the usual questions about the applicant's attitudes or values, such as commitment to hard work. Most people have rehearsed the answers they think employers want to hear. Instead, Starbucks utilizes questions about personal work experience to reveal actual behavior. A typical interview question at Starbucks may be something like, "Tell me a time when you had a conflict with someone at your last job and how you resolved it."

Likewise, we can consider Jesus trustworthy because of His behavior, thereby placing our faith in His promises. Although the Scriptures are alive with images of the divine attributes of Jesus, we can gather even more insight from His encounters with actual people, including women. This leaves us with the question: What does Jesus' relationships with the people He knew on earth tell us about Him? More specifically, how did Jesus build trust with the women He encountered?

Perhaps Jesus never expected those outside of His disciples to trust Him instinctively. Many didn't believe He was God who came in human form to dwell among creation on earth. This truth would be far too overwhelming for the average citizen to understand. As the Son of Man, His plan was to build credibility with the people He met by demonstrating His unwavering faithfulness.

Individuals in ancient Mediterranean culture faced trust issues similar to those in our society today. People felt trapped in circumstances beyond their control. Scripture's stories contain every form of hopeless situation, from disease and poverty to violence and corruption. According to some historians,

> ...people searched for security, looking for someone or something [upon] [whom] they [could] rely, to which they could pay their allegiance, upon which they [could] base their hope. Both trust and hope became a value that served as a means to attaining an honorable existence, so long as the source is trustworthy and reliable.[3]

For the average person, every day was a crisis or an

attempt at survival. Women were especially vulnerable and their circumstances often victimized them. In ancient Israel, a woman's status was inferior to a man's. Often, they were considered second-class citizens and scarcely above the status of slaves. Women were given little authority and were mostly restricted to their homes. They were subject to the men in their life, either their husbands or fathers.

Amazingly, Jesus broke the gender barrier of His time. The Gospels clearly portray Him as earning the trust of every woman He met. He saw them as worthy of honor and respect. He offered a safe place for women to experience healing, love, and forgiveness in His presence. The stories of Jesus' relationship with the women He encountered demonstrate that He can be relied on as our starting point, our *somewhere*. Like holding a finely cut diamond up to a light, we see facets of Jesus' divine character revealed in His interactions with the women He met. The eternal components of Jesus' love and unfathomable personality cannot be measured. Though immeasurable, we can identify a few of Jesus' personality traits that are important for trusting Him with our lives.

Let's start with compassion. Jesus' empathetic nature was evident to all those He met. According to Jesus' disciple Matthew, Jesus was intentional to reach out to individuals in need: "But when He saw the multitudes, He was moved with compassion for them, because they were weary and scattered, like sheep having no shepherd" (Matthew 9:36). He welcomed the outcasts who were ostracized by society, evident in the story of His encounter with a woman who was suffering for 12 years from chronic hemorrhaging. According to Jewish law, she was ceremonially unclean because of her condition. She was untouchable. Moreover, anyone coming into contact with her would also be considered unclean. However, Jesus saw something greater in her than a list of symptoms. He saw something so remarkable in this woman that she caught His attention and caused Him to turn around. In His eyes, she was not a victim of suffering. She was a woman of faith! Jesus not only healed her condition, but He also gave her a new life.

This story brings to mind a woman in my Berkeley neighborhood named Moesha, a battle-worn drug addict well into her 50s. She would often keep us awake by shouting obscenities as she paced back and forth on the sidewalk in front of our house. Occasionally, she would rest on the top step of our front stoop while continuing her verbal rampage. On a couple of occasions during the day, she arrived unexpectedly at my front door and snapped at me, ordering me to get out of "her" house. Unfortunately, she refused all of my offers to help her.

When Moesha was a little girl, she never imagined her

future as a drug addict. She never thought of herself one day pacing the street helplessly in the middle of the night. If she was remotely typical of most little girls, she had a dream. Perhaps she envisioned herself as an elementary school teacher, a recording artist, fashion model, or physician, but only God knows.

What went wrong? My guess is that somehow along the way, something really terrible, unthinkable, and traumatic happened to cause her dream to die. Moreover, she never experienced what she really needed most: hope for her future.

Yet, when Jesus looks at Moesha, he does not see a drug addict, prostitute, or hapless victim of life on the street. He sees her with eyes full of love as a beautiful woman full of purpose and potential. Moreover, He sees the high calling He has placed on her life as "His workmanship." The good news: Jesus is ready to bring hope and compassion and to set free all of the Moeshas who are crying out to Him.

If Jesus transformed the marginalized in His time on earth, how much more can we know that He is the same Jesus who serves as our compassionate high priest caring for us? He has provided a special place where we can meet with Him 24-7: His presence. The author of Hebrews identifies this Holy Place as the "throne of grace."

For we do not have a High Priest who cannot sympathize with our weaknesses, but was in all *points* tempted as *we are, yet* without sin. Let us therefore come boldly to the throne of grace, that we may obtain mercy and find grace to help in time of need (Hebrews 4:15-16).

Jesus' overflowing compassion toward Moesha qualifies him as trustworthy. He will treat us all as He treated her.

In addition to compassion, *Jesus was all about grace.* The companion to Jesus' deep compassion is His forgiveness, as we see throughout the Scriptures. Wherever He went, Jesus had a habit of forgiving people who didn't deserve it. He couldn't help it. His nature was to offer grace to those who needed it. He dispensed His mercy to all of the women He met. For example, in the Gospel of John we find a story of a woman caught in adultery by a group of religious leaders. She was practically dragged to Jesus. The religious leaders were trying to stone her, and they were just waiting for Jesus' permission. The leaders didn't even mention the man involved in the relationship, which indicates a double standard in the gender economy of that time.

The self-righteous religious leaders were unprepared for what Jesus did next. He ignored them. He did not pass judgment on the guilty woman. Instead, using His finger, He mysteriously began writing in the sand. I have always been curious about what He wrote. Of course we don't know, but we do know that Jesus publicly confronted the sin police of His day by calling them out: "He who is without sin among you, let him throw a stone at her first" (John 8:7).

After the embarrassed religious leaders slowly walked away, Jesus comforted the woman who had been shamed by her accusers, reassuring her: "Neither do I condemn you; go and sin no more" (John 8:11). Although we do not know if the woman knew anything about Jesus, she was aware of one thing. Jesus was someone who did not judge her, and even more amazingly, He was someone who forgave her and set her free. The woman may have needed to "go and sin no more" by patching up her relationship with her husband, but the important thing was that Jesus gave her another start. She was forgiven.

Like the unfaithful woman in John chapter 8, many people struggle to be free from the "adultery" of their past—those mistakes or sins that we long to leave behind. Unfortunately, like the religious leaders of Jesus' day, the condemning voices in our own minds are busy judging and gathering stones to throw at us. These voices can be more difficult to silence than actual people.

While such condemning voices are always trying to shame us for past sins, Jesus is always forgiving. The same

Jesus who forgave the woman thousands of years ago is ready to forgive us. Jesus told the woman then and he tells us today: "Neither do I condemn you; go and sin no more." His primary message to the woman was "Go." In other words, we are free to move on with our lives. We need not park in the place where we went wrong. The power of Jesus' forgiveness, quite evident throughout His encounters with women in the Gospel naratives, continues to be available to us as well.

As we turn the diamond of Jesus' character, we find a third characteristic reflected in His person: *He always told the truth.*

I am grateful to be married to a person I can trust, who loves me and is relentlessly devoted to me. Yet, my husband has an annoying habit: He tells me the truth. I am not referring to criticism or emotional abuse. On the contrary, he is very affectionate, encouraging, and constantly affirming his love for me. However, Earl will tell me the unvarnished truth about myself. Doubtless you are familiar with the cliché: "Does this (skirt, dress, pants, etc.) make me look too fat?" I am convinced that I am not the only woman who relies on her husband to be a secret girlfriend when it comes to fashion advice. On those important occasions when I need to look put together, I can count on Earl to be honest with me.

Yet for me, truth is something I don't always appreciate. Facing the truth is like sampling the dinner buffet at the Golden Corral. Some items that look extremely appetizing—fried shrimp, mashed potatoes, and prime rib—will always end up on my plate. I can do without some of the other items, like melting red Jell-O topped with Cool Whip, the messy chocolate fountain, or liquid cottage cheese with canned peaches on the side. Like sorting out the food I want to eat at a buffet, being open to the truth all depends on what I want to hear. For example, I am happy to take advice on trivial matters, like the best route to avoid heavy traffic into Seattle. But if the advice is personal—not so much. Nonetheless, someone who loves me enough to be honest with me is someone I can trust.

Jesus is all truth wrapped in a person. He was intentional about exposing the truth to everyone He encountered. As an example of Jesus' truth encounters, let's meet up with a lonely woman at a well. In the Gospel of John, we find a unique story about a woman who embraced the truth as her friend, though perhaps not at first.

The narrative begins when Jesus, weary from His journey, approaches a lonely Samaritan woman for a drink of water. Little does she know that her life will never be the same after her encounter with this stranger. She was probably surprised that He would even talk to her. A Jewish rabbi reaching out to a woman in public was unprecedented, especially if the woman was a Samaritan. The religious culture of the day frowned on associating with the outcast Samaritan community. In first-century Israel, Jews and Samaritans despised one another. Jews even avoided using dishes that Samaritans had used. Samaritans, and especially Samaritan women, were considered unclean. A Jewish person who drank from a Samaritan woman's vessel would also become ceremonially unclean.

As usual, Jesus stepped outside of the rigid religious box of His day. When He peered into the lonely, empty life of this woman, He loved her enough to confront her with the truth. All of it. The truth of her marital status. The truth about her previous five husbands. The truth that she was not married to the person with whom she was currently living. Jesus understood the compound pain she carried from all of her broken relationships. Next to the death of a loved one, divorce is the most traumatic emotional earthquake that can happen to a person. Instead of offering this hurting woman a bullet list of 10 ways to overcome a broken marriage, He gave her something better — His unfathomable love. He loved her enough to tell her the truth and to offer her the Living Water she so desperately needed.

Never underestimate the power of the truth to change your life. In the same manner as with the Samaritan woman,

Jesus loves us too much *not* to be honest and forthright with us.

I love cosmetics. Lipstick, eye shadow, mascara—I can't get enough. Cosmetics are fun! I especially find makeup useful for improving my appearance. Recently, I used a product called Master Concealer to hide the dark circles under my eyes. I have to say it works pretty well. However, it made me think of how people can become "Master Concealers" when we try to cover up our secrets and the hidden parts of us that we don't want to expose to the truth.

Jesus came to reach out to us in the places we need Him most, the places where we try to hide. We don't have to be afraid to trust Jesus with our secrets. He promises that "If we confess our sins, He is faithful and just to forgive us *our* sins and to cleanse us from all unrighteousness" (I John 1:9).

The truth that sets us free is the same truth that enables us to trust again. Like the Samaritan woman who finally let down her guard in the presence of Jesus, we can restore our trust as we begin to understand the truth, not as our enemy, but as our best friend.

I remember when I was the woman at the well who needed Jesus' living water. Although I wasn't a victim of divorce, I was tired of searching for a purpose for my life. At the time, I didn't realize how thirsty I was. It was this Jesus, this person of truth, I encountered the first time I began to read the New Testament. In reality, the Bible was reading me. It was at this moment that I knew God was real and that His Word was true.

Where do I begin to restore broken trust? One of my friends surveyed individuals who experienced trauma serving in overseas ministries. The common factor for those who overcame their crisis was their trust in God. We can trust God when we trade in negative experiences with people for God's truth.

Jesus' compassion, forgiveness, and truth endeared Him to the women He knew. Everywhere He went, regardless of their social or economic status, Jesus showed women kindness and respect. He publicly honored a poor widow who was willing to give all she had — only two mites (worth about one-eighth of a cent today). He praised her in front of His disciples, not only because He wanted to teach them a lesson on giving, but in order to raise her status from a poor woman to a rich person in God's eyes who had a specific purpose in the kingdom of God.

Follow their stories in the Gospels, and you will notice that in spite of their personal baggage, women leaned on Jesus when they could not trust anyone else. No need was too trivial for Jesus to meet. He even provided wine for a wedding on behalf of His own mother. Jesus earned the trust of the women He met, not only through the miracles He performed, but because women understood how much He loved them. His care, compassion, forgiveness, and respect for them transformed their lives. He was always willing to come visit the homes of His followers and perform miracles for women who were sick and suffering.

Suffice it to say, no one can be Jesus in your life. No person possesses the remarkable characteristics mirrored in this perfect person. Even His love cannot be contained. It fills the universe. Moreover, no individual has the immeasurable love toward you that Jesus can provide. The never-giving-up stubborn love that God has for us makes Him trustworthy.

Where do I go from here? Just weeks before we moved to California to start a church, we were visiting Berkeley when I tripped on a crack in a sidewalk and fell on my face. This fall resulted in deep cuts and a significant nose injury. Not surprisingly, I ended up in the emergency room at a nearby hospital, where a skilled Nurse Practitioner named Michael found me on a gurney. He began to sew the skin on the top of my nose together using a simple surgeon's tool: a needle and thread. Michael told us that he was tasked with helping me because of his skill with sutures. He had practiced on the skin of tomatoes.

During my recovery, I felt a strange mixture of emotions including shock, fear, and embarrassment. After several stitches, medication, and following the doctor's instructions to avoid sun exposure for six months, my wounded nose was eventually put back together, with the exception of a small bump that remains slightly visible.

In the same way that Michael sewed my nose together, Jesus came to be your physician. As Michael's skills with his suturing needle were instrumental in restoring my face, Jesus performed His miraculous healings on people as He walked the earth. For each woman He met, Jesus sewed together the places that were hurting and broken, making them beautiful.

For me, God's surgery of trust starts with the premise that God is good. Even if you have nothing else to go on, if you can believe that God is good in spite of your experiences, then you have something on which to cling. Start at that place. Start with the reality that, regardless of what your life looks like, God is good. You can then move forward in navigating the other challenges in your life.

When you learn to trust again, you experience healing power. I can embrace the stubborn hope that refuses to give in and refuses to let me live as a victim of my experiences. Hope happens in the process of letting go of the person who hurt you, and letting God take you by the hand and pulling you out of your hurt. Everyone needs to trust someone. We can learn to trust again because of who Jesus is and what He has done for us. I can put my trust in Jesus who never changes and who continues to be "...the same yesterday, today, and forever" (Hebrews 13:8).

A Prayer

Thank you Jesus that I can trust you.

Where others have failed me, you stand loyal and true.

I can trust you with my life, my hurts, and my challenges.

Help me to trust you more each day.

I give all of my expectations to you and not to others.

I'm letting go of all those who have disappointed me.

Restore my trust, not only in You Lord,

but in those who love me and want to be my friend.

Thank you for taking my hand, healing me,

and bringing me close to you.

Questions for Reflection

- Can you think of a person/persons from your past who betrayed your trust? How did those experiences affect your ability to trust in your relationships with others?
- Read Hebrews 4:14-16, 1 Peter 5:7, and John 15:1-13. What do you see as the major obstacle preventing you from trusting other people?

- List three character traits of Jesus that qualify Him as someone you can trust.
- What are some practical action steps you can take to overcome your trust issues?

Epilogue

You may be happy to know that I am feeling much more positive about my life since I began this book several months ago. Although I hoped I could be "zapped" into immediate wholeness, I see God's hand in my life in so many small ways.

The tall pines in my new backyard have been a constant form of therapy. Christian community has also been a continuing source of encouragement. I have been inspired by my pastor's sermons. He "nails it" by speaking into my life at every point of need.

My husband and my ministry friends have provided additional encouragement and have helped me put the pieces of my life back together. Along the way, God has brought me little fragments of hope in many ways, including through a friend from Oregon who came to visit and brought me two of her beautiful paintings to display in my home.

Just as spring has arrived in Washington after a long winter, I can see a new season of hope in which sunshine is taking over from a long winter of discouragement. For instance, my relationships with the female ministers in my area are blossoming.

I am developing a new point of view about the risk my husband and I took to start our California church, and this is giving me a new path forward. In the last few months, I no longer regret the bold decision we made, in spite of the disappointing outcome. I enjoy lasting relationships with some of the people who were part of our team, and I would not trade that for a high-profile position in a successful megachurch.

Many destinies changed as a result of the huge step we made to live in Berkeley. One married couple we stay in touch with actually met at our church when there were only a handful of people. Both of them were a part of our leadership, not knowing that they would one day fall in love and get married. They now have an adorable son and live in the East Bay. We still stay in touch with them through Facebook.

Recently, we have a new addition to our family. Buddy, a white West Highlands Terrier/Maltese mix came to us as a rescue dog from a local animal shelter. He is adjusting well to his role as Ricky's successor and seems to want to spend every minute of every day with me.

Among the tall pines, hope has returned to my life — not because of my own will power or by eating five cucumbers and day, but because Jesus is still God's best idea.

"Blessed *be* the God and Father of our Lord Jesus Christ, who according to His abundant mercy has begotten us again to a living hope through the resurrection of Jesus Christ from the dead, to an inheritance incorruptible and undefiled and that does not fade away, reserved in heaven for you"

(1 Peter 1:3-4).

NOTES

INTRODUCTION

1. *The Matrix Reloaded*, directed by the Wachowski Brothers, (Village Roadshow Productions, 2003).

2. Anne Lamott, *Bird by Bird: Some Instructions on Writing and Life* (New York: Anchor Books, 1994), xxiii.

CHAPTER 1

1. **1573** *ekkaké. Strong's Concordance.*
http://biblehub.com/greek/1573.htm

2. William Barclay, *The Gospel of Luke*. Rev. ed. (Philadelphia, PA: Westminster Press, 1975), 222.

3. Ibid., 222.

CHAPTER 2

1. Alan Nelson and Gene Appel, *How to Change Your Church Without Killing It* (Nashville, TN: Thomas Nelson, 2008), 14

CHAPTER 3

1. *The Walking Dead*, Directed by. Written by. AMC. (American Movie Classics)
Created bys Frank Darabont, Oct 31 2010 – present. Based on comic book series of the same name by Robert Kirkman, Tony Moore, Charlie Adlard.

2. *Strong's Concordance,*

http://biblehub.com/greek/5610.htm

5610 *hora* – properly, an *hour*; (figuratively) a *finite* "season"; *limited* time or opportunity to reach a goal (fulfill a purpose); a *divinely pre-set* time-period; a limited period to accomplish the Lord's specific purpose, i.e. "the hour" in which specific characteristics prevail exactly like that for a limited time.

CHAPTER 4

1. John A. Martin, "Luke," *The Bible Knowledge Commentary: New Testament.* Eds John F. Walvoord, Roy B. Zuck. (Wheaton, IL: Victor Books, 1983), 56.

CHAPTER 5

1. Jim Casey, "Carrie Underwood Reveals She Needed More than 40 Facial Stitches After Her Accident in November," *The Nash Country Daily*, January 2, 2018. http://www.nashcountrydaily.com/2018/01/02/carrie-underwood-reveals-she-needed-more-than-40-facial-stitches-after-her-accident-in-november/

2. Billy Graham Evangelistic Association, "Cliff Barrows: Profile," https://billygraham.org/about/biographies/cliff-barrows/

3. Taylor Swift in Ellie McVeigh, "My Favorite Singer," 17 March 2016. https://prezi.com/xjkr9v0s8plq/my-favorite-singer/?webgl=0

CHAPTER 6

1. Tini Heng, "I Started Eating Cucumber 3 Times A Day As The Doctor Said, After 5 days Something Changed," February 19, 2018 https://heavyload.com/started-eating-cucumber-3-times-day-doctor-said-3-days

CHAPTER 7

1. Stanley Toussaint, "Book of Acts." *The Bible Knowledge Commentary: New Testament.* Eds. John F. Walvoord and Roy B. Zuck. (Wheaton, IL: Victor Books), 399.

CHAPTER 8

1. "Mary Magdalene: The Woman Who Had Seven Devils." *All the Women of the Bible*, Vol. 2. https://www.biblegateway.com/resources/all-women-bible/Mary-Magdalene

2. *Strong's Concordance,* **2799** *klaí*☐ – properly, weep aloud, expressing uncontainable, audible grief ("audible weeping," WP, 2, 88). http://biblehub.com/greek/2799.htm

3. Mary Oaklander, "The Science of Crying." *Time.* March 16, 2016. http://time.com/collection/guide-to-happiness/4254089/science-crying/

4. Jonathan Rottenberg quoted in Oaklander. "The Science of Crying."

5. William Frey, in Ryan Bradley, "The Tears of Rose-Lynn Fisher." *Southwest: The Magazine* (August 2017), 50-56, 72-75. https://www.southwestmag.com/the-tears-of-rose-lynn-fisher/ Retreived April 7, 2018.

6. Oaklander, "The Science of Crying"

7. Bradley, "The Tears of Rose-Lynn Fisher."

8. Rose-Lynn Fisher in Bradley, "The Tears of Rose-Lynn Fisher."

9. Bradley, "The Tears of Rose-Lynn Fisher."

CHAPTER 9

1. Bruce Drake, "Six New Findings About Millennials." Pew Research Center. March 4, 2014.
http://www.pewresearch.org/fact-tank/2014/03/07/6-new-findings-about-millennials/

2. Connie Cass, "Poll: Americans Don't Trust One Another." *USA Today*, November 30, 2013.
https://www.usatoday.com/story/news/nation/2013/11/30/poll-americans-dont-trust-one-another/3792179/

3. John J. Pilch and Bruce Malina, eds. "Trust (Personal and Group)", *Handbook of Biblical Social Values*. 3rd ed. (Eugene, OR: Cascade Books, 2016), 173.

ABOUT THE AUTHOR

Dr. Janet Creps, a native of Wisconsin, has a background as both a musician and professional artist. She and her husband Earl have pastored four churches, including a church plant in Berkeley, California.

Janet has been a speaker at conferences and retreats for women, married couples, missionaries, and college students. She is also a published author.

Janet completed both her Master of Divinity and Doctor of Ministry degrees at the Assemblies of God Theological Seminary. She is an ordained minister with the Assemblies of God and has served as a nationally appointed home missionary with US Missions.

Janet's hobbies include writing, cooking, watching old black and white movies, taking train rides and long scenic road trips, and drinking great coffee.

Janet and her husband Earl live in Redmond, Washington.

Made in the USA
San Bernardino, CA
14 July 2018